P9-AOB-670
.A799
D72
1990

RAGONS & DEMONS, ANGELS & EAGLES

Morality Tales for Teens

Brother Stephen Chappell, O.S.B.

SALZMANN LIBRARY
St. Francis Seminary
3257 South Lake Drive
St. Francis, Wis. 53235

Imprimi Potest:
James Shea, C.SS.R.
Provincial, St. Louis Province
The Redemptorists

Imprimatur:
Monsignor Maurice F. Byrne
Vice Chancellor, Archdiocese of St. Louis

ISBN 0-89243-314-0
Library of Congress Catalog Card Number: 89-63202

Copyright © 1990, Bro. Stephen Anthony Chappell, O.S.B.
Printed in U.S.A.

All rights reserved. No part of this book may be reproduced, stored
in a retrieval system, or transmitted without the written permission
of Liguori Publications.

Scripture selections are taken from the NEW AMERICAN BIBLE WITH
REVISED NEW TESTAMENT, copyright © 1986, by the Confraternity
of Christian Doctrine, Washington, DC 20017, and are used by
permission of copyright owner. All rights reserved.

Cover and interior art: Chris Sharp

This book is lovingly dedicated to my parents, who have been so enthusiastic and supportive; Brother Anselm (Keith) Williams, who has been of such help with his critiques and encouragement; and Bryan, who by virtue of having a copy of the original manuscript in his safekeeping saved me an unbelievable amount of work. Above all, this work is dedicated to my students at Columbia Catholic School with whom I have shared these tales, particularly the members of the class of 1987, who were the inspiration for the tales. I especially dedicate this book to Chris, whose belief in this project saw me through some frustrating times. It was for all of you that this work was undertaken, and it is to you that it forever belongs.

"Bro' "

CONTENTS

Introduction   7

The Pilgrim and the Monk *(Prologue)*   9

    I. Turn and Perdir 14

   II. The Forest of the Soul's Mirror 23

  III. Olu of the Yorubas 33

  IV. The Eaglet 41

   V. Thaïx the Dragon 48

  VI. Judgment Day 56

 VII. The Sins of the Fathers 65

VIII. The Visitor 75

  IX. Hannah of Soroki 84

  X. The Mighty Gorm 95

The Tale of Small and Deep *(Epilogue)* 103

Appendix: Scriptural and Theological Commentaries
  on the Tales 107

INTRODUCTION

Of the many ways to teach, few are so hallowed as the art of storytelling. The oldest parts of the Bible began as campfire stories told by the early Hebrews in the days before they learned the art of writing. To keep their faith alive the Hebrews would pass along truth to their young ones in the only form available to them: the story. Ever since, the story has always been a favorite form of entertainment and learning for young and old. The tales in this book began as oral stories. In an attempt to vary my teaching techniques at Columbia Catholic School where I have taught for some years, I tried to spark discussion by inventing and telling stories with moral lessons. Some of those stories are contained here. It was through the encouragement of my students that I put them in written form, and the result is before you.

This book can be used in several ways. You can read it straight through like a book no different from any other. By using the conversations of Gershom and the pilgrim as a setting, you can read this as a novel. Or these stories can be retold aloud. That would be best, for that is how they began. I kept the dialogues of Gershom and the pilgrim independent of each story so as not to interfere with the possibility of using a particular story that fits a use in a classroom or retreat setting. Finally, there is an appendix at the end that includes scriptural reflections for further study and meditation. These reflections are for those wishing to use these tales as a means to spur spiritual growth and familiarity with Bible themes.

If the stories limp in their style, it is the fault of the author, who has never dabbled in the art of writing before. But it is my prayerful hope that in these tales there may be something of value for you, your class, or your retreat group. May these stories help you build and strengthen your own faith and make you aware of the loving goodness of God and the oneness that we who believe share with Jesus Christ, our Lord.

Peace!

Br. Stephen, OSB

Columbia, Missouri

THE PILGRIM
AND THE MONK

(PROLOGUE)

HE wind that eddied about the ridge was warm and dry. Still as a heron that sensed an unseen presence, a man stood gazing across a chasm to the opposite ridge that was slightly higher than where he was. *Montserrat!* The ancient monastery was, at long last, before him. It perched on a perilous ledge near the mountaintop, a place as fabled as it was ancient. This pilgrim had reached his goal and lost himself in thought for the moment. He had come as a pilgrim to this great abbey, hoping against hope for answers to countless questions and peace for a troubled heart. He murmured a prayer to Our Lady of Montserrat that he would find here what he had traveled far to find.

It had been a long journey to get here, both in distance and in time. He had been to other shrines, perhaps more famous than Montserrat, but the healing he had found at them had been for needs other than his own, or so it seemed.

How much longer must I search? he wondered.

The world he lived in spun too dizzyingly fast. Truths of yesterday that he had grown up with seemed to vanish like mist in the daylight of the present, and old certainties seemed like so many dreams. He felt confused. All he wanted was something to anchor his life, something to make it all worth living for. In his heart he wanted truth that would see him through a life that seemed an enemy to faith, but he always felt like a fool for having made the effort. And yet the pilgrim still felt the need to believe in *something* in spite of the struggle he'd had. *I am no person of faith,* the pilgrim had told himself too many times, but he nonetheless fought to keep faith from dying within him.

In the rainbowed interior of the great cathedral at Chartres, the pilgrim had touched faith with his soul, yet lacked the wisdom to hold onto it or a guide to show him how. Faith faded from his grasp again, and he went on…looking, struggling. Neither the great centers of pilgrimage nor the simple little pieties of the people he met along the way seemed able to fill his need or help him. He was despairing of the whole search and about to dismiss it all as foolishness when, not long before the present moment, he chanced on a tourist's picture book of the Abbey of Montserrat. Something, something he could not name, whispered to him, "Go! Seek! Ask, and it shall be there that you will find what you are after."

And so he had made his way to Montserrat, leaving his car and comforts in obedience to an inexplicable instinct to do so. He had made his way as a true pilgrim: hiking, hitching a ride when the weather was poor, and sleeping in the open…all in response to some deep, voiceless drive within him.

Now here he was in Spain.

"Marvelous," he said aloud. "Now what?"

Dusty and shaggy, he stood at the precipice. He looked ragged and thoroughly tired, and yet, oddly, he also felt radiant. The fading afternoon sun gilded the ancient abbey, erasing all traces of time. Generation had followed generation, and hundreds of monks had found the answers to their own searching here at long-honored Montserrat. Excitement shivered through the pilgrim's body, bracing him. Could his search end here?

"Magnificent, is it not, my brother?"

The pilgrim jumped. Seeing only the monastery in its breathtaking setting, he had overlooked a monk sitting beneath the wind-gnarled tree behind him. The monk sat cross-legged in his brown habit. His hood shadowed most of his face, but from beneath the shadow his eyes sparkled merrily. A slight but clearly amused smile betrayed the comedy he found in having startled the pilgrim. Large but elegant hands and sandaled feet were all that did not blend into the shade beneath the tree, so it had been quite easy for the pilgrim to overlook him.

I could've sworn there had been no one under the tree when I arrived! the pilgrim thought.

The monk spoke, pulling back his hood from a gentle face, "Forgive me, I did not mean to give you a fright." The voice reverberated deep and yet strangely melodic all at once. "I came up here, as you did, to meditate. I am called Gershom."

To the pilgrim the name did not sound Spanish or anything close to it, so he quickly decided that the monk was, like himself, a pilgrim.

"How...how do you do? You really took me by surprise! Are you a monk of here, of Montserrat, I mean?" he asked with a nod toward the abbey.

"Oh, no, my brother," the deep voice purred. "As you may have guessed," he said with a knowing glint in his eye, "I am, like yourself, a wayfarer." He paused, considering something. "And what brings you to holy Montserrat?"

The pilgrim, for no good reason that he could understand, began to open his heart to its core and poured out his story and pain to the monk. It was not until the pilgrim had finished that the monk, leaning back thoughtfully against the tree trunk, spoke.

"You have done well to follow your heart here, my friend, for I assure you that you did not just wander here; you were led. Montserrat, rich in tradition and history, powerful in prayer, will be the end of your search. Although, I doubt it will be as a monk. Your coming to Montserrat was a test for your sincerity."

The monk rose and walked, nearly seeming to glide across the terrain. The pilgrim's puzzled eyes followed him to the edge of the rocks and then looked pensively at the great monastery. Dusk was falling about them, and the warm glow of lights began to fill Montserrat's many windows.

"Montserrat," the monk murmured in a prayerful tone as he addressed the abbey, "How very much like L'Chabra-dìa you are."

"L'Chabra-dìa?" the pilgrim echoed.

The monk turned and studied the pilgrim for a moment, then resumed his cross-legged posture with his back to the darkening sky.

"Many years ago," he said in a voice that seemed to make his words like a personal memory, "when the Christian message was yet new, it took root in a kingdom of the East. In that land where East and West meet, that message was embraced and cherished and, like fruit on a sturdy tree, was nurtured and enriched. In few places did the faith ripen so well as in that land. But it was astride ancient trade routes, and alas! The very conditions that made the land so prosperous and so blessed also proved her undoing. Armies swept across her borders, back and forth, pillaging and destroying. Beneath the heels of conquerors and bandits it is still torn apart between rival countries to this day. Yet, before that happened, a group of her people who were particularly devoted to the faith escaped the ruin of their country and found a place of refuge deep in the mighty Caucasus Mountains. In a high valley, sheltered from the northern winds, they built their fortress city of L'Chabra-dìa.

"The name is said to mean a place of haven, and so it has been. Within their walls rose the Glass Tower where, atop its pinnacle, in a room that commanded a view of all the valley, there was the Peacock Throne. The guardian of L'Chabra-dìa sat on that throne watching over the borders of the land with farseeing eye. Known to the outside world only as He Who Sleeps Not, he was the unresting watcher who is as legendary as L'Chabra-dìa itself. Some say that he had eyes that blazed with the light of twin suns. Some say he was the apostle John, immortal and waiting for the return of his Lord. Others say he was not one man but a series of nameless elders, wise and powerful. And still others say that he was...more.

"But as long as He Who Sleeps Not watched over L'Chabra-dìa, there was peace. And in that peace, wisdom grew. Like the cherished jewels that were left to the world by the great master of the parable — the Nazorean — the lore of L'Chabra-dìa has been occasionally shared with the outside world, shared in the form of The Tales."

"The Tales? Go on; please tell me more." The pilgrim had become enchanted by the monk's story.

The monk smiled; his audience was now a captive one. He replied, "Faith is built upon a foundation of truth, and that foundation is made of the Word, the eternal Word. Would you, my brother, wish to find and own this faith for yourself? *The* faith that has seen countless numbers through an otherwise confusing life?"

"Yes, oh yes! It is what I have come all this way to find!" The pilgrim nearly cried the words.

The evening air grew still. From somewhere a flickering light reflected itself in the right eye of the monk's now darkened face. Suddenly, parallel to that reflection, the evening star sprang into silver fire, illuminating his left eye as well. "Then if you would own faith, you must first know the truth, and to know truth you must first hear the Word. Listen well to these words, and you will hear the Word underlying them. These, Pilgrim, are The Tales from L'Chabra-dìa."

And with that, the monk began....

1.

TURN AND
PERDIR

N the vast plains of central Asia rose the city of the Astrakar: the People of the Stars, so-called for the millions of stars one could see in the night sky above their quiet, shining city. For centuries the Astrakar made their fortune by outfitting the great caravans that carried fine goods between imperial Constantinople in the west to the cities of distant China toward the sunrise. In the troubled Middle Years, Mongol hordes overran their city, and the Astrakar scattered, dwindled, and then altogether disappeared; but until that time they dwelt in relative peace, far removed from the great doings in the lands to the south.

The Astrakar had amassed a great store of wise traditions handed down since days no longer remembered. Far from neighboring peoples and a close-knit folk by nature, the Astrakar grew together in a way that was less national than it was kindly, held by the heritage they shared and the ancient faith that gave them purpose.

In the years before the first sack of Rome and the start of the great troubles for the peoples of the West, two sons were born to neighboring families on the same day. Turn and Perdir grew up together, fast friends who shared dreams of the future when they, too, would join the great caravans and see the wonders of faraway places. Indeed, so close were these two that people frequently took them to be brothers. In the boys' earlier years, people often had to stop and think before being sure which boy they were speaking to, so alike were Turn and Perdir.

As they grew toward manhood, however, noticeable differences appeared, as they have a way of doing. Most were small things, not important in-and-of themselves. But of the differences that distinguished the two, the most noticeable and disturbing one was their differing attitudes toward the Faith and the time-honored ritual of "The Bonding."

The Bonding was a ceremony in which all of the Astrakar gathered to both witness and bless their young people as they reached adulthood. Men and women alike received The Bonding on the dawn of the days that marked a new season of the year. The teachers of the Faith said that no Astrakim (as a single member of their people was called) who received The Bonding could ever be lost to the Astrakar and would belong to their people forever. What this meant had so long been a matter of sacred fact that, at length, no one really knew exactly what The Bonding *did*, but all agreed that it was extremely important and solemn. Above all, The Bonding had to be a matter of free choice. Participants in The Bonding had to give their consent before all the witnessing Astrakar; therefore, the people regarded The Bonding as a sign of commitment to the Astrakar way of life as well. Although there were those who did not choose The Bonding, they usually left for other lands, and by far the greater part of the Astrakar were those among the ranks of "The Bound."

Turn had always looked forward to becoming one of The Bound, but it was not so with Perdir. To him the term only spoke of entrapment into a way of life that he found boring, at best. The Astrakar were a happy people, as full of joy as the sparkling starlight that gave them their name, but it was a quiet joy of simple pleasures and living a life based on upright living and good deeds to their neighbors. Although they traveled far in their caravans, the Astrakar's journeying was looked upon as a necessary evil for the support of their people. They shared all things, and for one of The Bound, the best part of a journey was the return home to be among their people again.

Perdir could see no obvious advantage that The Bonding gave to those who accepted it. It did impose restrictions and responsibilities, tying one to the Astrakar and seemingly shutting off the marvelous world outside, save for what could be seen of it by traveling with the great caravans. Worse still, Perdir reasoned, The Bound behaved strangely. They shunned many of the pleasures that the world held out to them and instead took joy in the most commonplace, trivial things. They and their city bored Perdir, and he yearned for the day when he would be old enough to join one of the caravans and escape the suffocating embrace of his home city.

Turn could not understand his companion's attitudes any more than Perdir could understand Turn's attitudes, yet the two maintained their friendship steadfastly and took great care not to nag each other. After all, The Bonding had to be accepted freely and with no coercion or it would have no effect.

So it was that on the first day of autumn in the year of their maturity that the two youths became eligible for The Bonding and full adult membership in the community. Turn joyfully accepted...but not Perdir. He remained unmoved by the grave concern that he saw in the eyes of his family, the tears of love and nameless fear that hung there. They, for their part, remained silent, never speaking a word against his decision. They could not force their son, and in the wisdom of their people Perdir's family knew that only Perdir could choose a change of heart. If time worked such a change, he might yet receive The Bonding at a later time.

So on a clear, crisp morning just before the dawn, Turn and his peers underwent The Bonding. The last of the night's stars and his people stood by as witnesses. Surrounded by The Bound — who

rhythmically chanted the ancient songs that belonged to the ceremony — the newcomers recited ritual lines, made their pledges
before the Astrakar and The Power That Lies Behind All, and
submitted themselves to be anointed with fragrant oils.

The joyous sounds of the celebration carried far beyond the city
walls, but their echoes did not reach Perdir. He stood alone, far out
on the empty plain, staring gloomily into the rising sun and feeling
a vague regret that angered him. His only companion was a grave
foreboding; but of what, he did not know.

❊ ❊ ❊

Having reached adulthood, both young men now needed to
choose a life's work to support themselves and their way of life. It
came as no surprise, since it had been their mutual dream since
childhood, that both chose to join themselves to one of the caravans
that were the lifeblood flowing through the city of the Astrakar.

Their years became a record of countless miles of travel between
misty Europe and the mysterious East. Both young men worked
with untiring devotion to their labors; yet, despite the history of
friendship between them, a gap increasingly separated them from
each other. Turn was quiet, calm, peaceful, uncritical, not given to
cheap or mean laughter, and generous to a fault. In short, he
modeled all that an Astrakim should be.

Not so Perdir! His temper could strike out at man, beast, or thing
without distinction or warning. His values were worldly by the
standards of the Astrakar. Rumors circulated about his doings in
the places and with the people he visited when the caravans stopped
in foreign cities. Astrakar heads shook and cast disapproving looks
on these jaunts of Perdir's. Yet no one lectured him, for to do so
merely ignited his temper and harsh words. He grumbled and
fretted constantly and seemed to hold his fellows (all, save for Turn)
in contempt. Yet he often sought out festivity and seemed in great

dread of being alone for very long. The vast, empty spaces of central Asia seemed to call forth a deep, nameless fear from within him. He slept poorly, often tormented by restless dreams. Turn often wondered what it was that seemed to torture his old friend Perdir. The older Astrakar, wise with the years of observing the world and its ways and how it dealt with the children of the earth, knowingly glanced at one another and sadly shook their heads.

The years whirled by in quick succession, riotous spring and summer giving way to warm glowing autumn and the end of the caravans for another year, over and over again. The two friends had now been to the shores of sunny Greece and had gazed upon the rocky, frozen towers that ringed forbidden Tibet. Common toil, adventure, and shared danger deepened their knowledge of each other, yet both could sense at the same time that an increasing gap, a gulf with no bridge, widened between them. Despite all that they shared, that eerie sense of separation remained.

❊ ❊ ❊

The shrouded sky was red with dawn the morning that the raiders appeared. Wending its way back from the East, the caravan was not far from home when it was attacked by the raiders on the banks of one of the rare rivers on Asia's vast central plains, not far removed from their home. Skin-clad horsemen armed with lances, bows, and arrows descended on the startled camp and raged among its ranks with mayhem and death.

Turn, never one very skilled with arms, snatched a firebrand from a campfire and fended off the attackers as best he could. Perdir, standing astride a fallen opponent, glanced over his shoulder to see his friend unseat a horseman with a strong swing of the firebrand. The horseman fell to the ground with a thud. As Turn raised his arm to deal another blow, a second horseman galloped by and struck Turn solidly across the skull with a club. Eyes wide,

Turn dropped to his knees and then fell face downward on the ground.

"Turn!" Perdir screamed in agony as though an arrow had pierced his very heart. He leaped toward the fallen, still form of Turn — taking two steps, then three, when a pain in his side made the earth spin and then swallowed up his consciousness in a grey fog that quickly surrendered to blackness.

The veiled sun set that evening on the smoldering remains of the camp. Here and there an odd form or two twitched about, but for the most part, the scene lay silent and still, especially where dead bodies dotted the ground.

✻ ✻ ✻

Perdir's eyes grew accustomed to the dim half-light. Confused, he reasoned that he must have been unconscious until well after twilight. And yet, where was he? And where was the camp? Had they packed and fled, leaving him behind for dead? "Turn? Turn!" he began calling for his friend, his voice echoing weirdly in the heavy mist that wrapped everything. The sickening pain that felled Perdir had gone away. He wondered why. He also had no wound that he could find, and this puzzled him too. Why was there no pain? Had he been unconscious that long?

He began to pace but quickly froze in mid-step. A hint of a movement swirled the mist, but he could neither see nor hear anything.

"Turn?" he asked, his body remaining motionless while his eyes darted all about. Whatever the movement in the mist was, it had turned away and retreated into the gloom. Now and then Perdir would catch a glimpse of motion from the corner of his eye, but each time he found nothing in the gloom that flanked him on all sides.

Time passed. Too much time, Perdir thought. Ought not the sun to rise and dispel the clinging mist? Despite his dashings about, he felt neither tired nor hungry nor thirsty…and Perdir had never been accustomed to going for very long without food or drink. A chill gripped Perdir at the thought. All his life he had never gone so long without feeling the pangs of hunger or thirst. Why did he not feel the need for food or drink now?

Again, the motion caught his eye.

His eyes chased it once more, but in vain. Like a will-o'-the-wisp it eluded him without any inkling of who or what it might be. It could not be Turn, surely, but whoever or whatever it was, Perdir wished it would tell him where he was, just *talk* to him.

Then a thirst did begin to burn in Perdir, not for water but for company. He yearned for the sound of another human voice to ease the oppressive, hateful gloom — to keep him from feeling so lonely. *Lonely*. The word hung, trembling in his mind. *Alone*. Perdir was alone. Suddenly he realized where he was, why the sun would never rise, and that he would never catch the phantom shapes.

ALONE!

The word beat like a pounding drum. With a soul-wrenching sob the man sank to his knees and began to weep bitterly.

❋ ❋ ❋

Turn was a long time recovering from the blow he had been dealt. The Astrakar had beaten their attackers but not without heavy losses. It was not until they had the young man safely back in their city and well on the way to recovery that they could bring themselves to tell Turn about the burying of his childhood companion far out on the plains. Turn grieved for a great while, but in due time his life moved onward. Many more caravan seasons awaited him and, in time, he married, raised a family and, at the end of a long life full of happiness and golden memories, passed on.

But for Turn there would be no land of gloomy mists after his death. As he passed down the long tunnel of darkness leading from this life to the next, he beheld at its end a light of staggering brightness. It sparkled in the distance before him and then, with a dazzling rush of brilliance, it enfolded him. He found himself standing among other Astrakar, all greeting him with open arms. But these Astrakar were all friends and relatives long passed from the world. These were The Bound who had departed life and, linked by the vows of The Bonding, were spending eternity in blessed, joyful company.

Happy the fate of Turn! One with the joyful Bound, never to know loneliness or the pain of separation again. His was the happy choice, the choice that led to life always. And more beloved Astrakar came to join Turn and the others as the world made its way until, in the world, the Astrakar were no more.

In the dark, Gershom the monk paused.

"Tell me, Pilgrim, what have you learned about faith from the tale of Turn and Perdir?"

The pilgrim thought a moment before replying. "I have learned," he began slowly, "that sometimes faith is a trust you place in things you don't fully understand. Things don't always make sense in this world, but we have to trust that there are powers who know more than we do at times, and we have to follow what those powers instruct, even if others think we're foolish. It may even mean denying ourselves things that others consider harmless and desirable. It means trusting in a wisdom greater and older than our own understanding." The pilgrim paused to lick his lips and then asked, "Is that it, Gershom? Is that what faith is all about?"

In the dark, the monk smiled. The pilgrim learned quickly, and that was good.

"It is *part* of what faith is all about, Pilgrim," Gershom replied. "But that is not *all* there is to it. Consider, if you will, the following," and with that he began another tale....

II.

THE FOREST OF THE SOUL'S MIRROR

AHOUL was a merchant in the city of Tabriz. Indeed, Fahoul was *the* merchant of Tabriz — wealthy as few were and powerful to the point of rivaling kings. Throughout the city and the surrounding region all knew the name of Fahoul, and word of his great wealth carried far and wide. His caravans traveled to Greece, Baghdad, and even legendary India. His ships plied the great landlocked Caspian Sea. For their projects and monuments the mighty caliphs themselves sent fawning messengers from Baghdad to borrow money from the wealthy Fahoul. Fahoul's considerable fame was only heightened by people's knowledge of the humble beginnings from which he had climbed.

But as many as there were who sang Fahoul's praises, they did so only because of his great wealth. There were many who also whispered darkly of how he had achieved it. His beginnings were indeed humble; his father was a shoemaker who by hard work had earned a decent living, putting aside a modest amount for his later years. Fahoul was his only child — a son who shared his father's determination and thrift yet somehow lacked his father's simple decency. Early in life Fahoul had shown others that when he was forced to choose between money and people, people would always come out on the losing end of the encounter. It was his father who, persuaded by Fahoul, financed his son's first trading venture from his savings for his own old age. The venture was successful and turned a handsome profit for Fahoul. But Fahoul never returned any of the money to his father, claiming that the loan was his inheritance. He instead outfitted a new venture and left for better opportunity in Tabriz. His father died heartbroken and penniless some years later.

Were this not bad enough, Fahoul loaned money to a widowed cousin in Tabriz who, with her children, had no kin there, save for him alone. It would have been better if they had no one! When she was unable to repay the loan at the required time, he foreclosed, seizing all that she had and casting her from her home. With no feeling for the distress he had already put upon his poor relative, he even sold her children into slavery, unintentionally sparing them a worse fate. Their mother starved to death in the streets of Tabriz.

It was by such means that Fahoul had built his wealth into a mountain, and the gutters of Tabriz were home to many whom he had sent there. For every voice that sang his praises, there were two cursing the day of his birth. Yet fortune seemed to smile on Fahoul, and no evil ever so much as clouded his days. The wealthy sought his company, while the ambitious pursued his support, and all the while his wealth grew. No reverses ever came to make him repent of his greed and cruelty, and his ruthlessness mounted as quickly as his piles of gold.

Such was his life on the eve of his journey to the shores of the Caspian. Fahoul had grown suspicious of the chief overseer in charge of the goods that Fahoul's ships carried upon the great inland sea. Profits had been down from their usual levels, and Fahoul entertained the question of whether it might not be the fault of his overseer. Honesty was a virtue Fahoul prized highly in others, and so he decided to see, unannounced, whether it was a virtue that his overseer practiced too. Alone, for the roads were safe at the time,

Fahoul set out. He had craftily let out word that he intended to journey to Baghdad and enjoy the pleasures of the capital so that no one would send word to his overseer. He set out early but just beyond Tabriz took the eastward road toward the sea.

After several days' travel through the mountainous country, the road opened onto the mountain end of a wide canyon, winding down to where the canyon mouth met the flat, narrow coastal plain. Gulls wheeled and called overhead, and on the far horizon Fahoul could see the line of deeper blue that was the great Caspian Sea. Between him and it lay nothing but the plain that was featureless except for a nearly circular smudge of grey-green known only as "The Forest."

Fahoul had been this way only once before, many years back when he bought his first few ships. His guide at the time, a native of the region, brought him along the very same road that met the abrupt, sharply-defined edge of The Forest. It was an edge that defined itself so sharply it seemed unnatural. The road ran up to The Forest's very shadows only to veer aside and skirt it on the south. Fahoul remembered the weather-worn sign that someone had posted there. In darkly stained letters it read:

The Forest of the Soul's Mirror
Let only he who knows himself well enter here.

Fahoul had asked his guide what the sign meant. The man, glancing nervously into the dark woods, muttered something about none but the good ever passing through the woods with either life or mind intact. Vaguely, Fahoul recalled bits of legends and superstitions that the guide had bored him with as they skirted the looming trees. None of the tales were very definite except on one point: There was something decidedly unhealthy about or in The Forest, and one would be wise to stay out of it at all costs.

The stories made even less of an impression on Fahoul now as he reined his horses down the canyon road toward the plain. The bright morning drifted by.

It was nearly midday when Fahoul approached the western edge of The Forest. From a distance he could spot the same forbidding sign shadowed beneath the grey twisted trees. Although he rode at perfect ease, the nearer to the trees that he came, the more skittish his horse became. She began to roll her eyes, and her ears flattened back as if she were alert to a menace sensed but not seen. Fahoul had little regard for the wisdom of beasts, nor did he recall the nervousness of the mounts that he and his guide rode the first time he had laid eyes upon The Forest. However, an occasional lion could still be found in these parts, so he reined the mare to a halt and stood up in the stirrups, peering into the gloom.

Suddenly the horse reared! Fahoul tumbled off, striking his head as he tumbled. With a shrill whinny, the horse wheeled and galloped away, back toward the hills. She swiftly disappeared into the distance.

As Fahoul came around, he carefully picked himself up, aflame with rage and indignity, cursing the luckless mare. How long he had been unconscious he could not say, but he felt certain the horse would be heading home toward Tabriz. He would have the ill-bred nag whipped upon his return, he thought. But in the meantime Fahoul feared that someone might find her and recognize her as his horse. There might be a possible search that could give his overseer alarm, costing him the element of surprise. He would reach the sea on foot long before the horse could possibly reach Tabriz, but he decided to hasten on and avoid even the chance. Fahoul had never been one to gamble unless the odds were highly in his favor. The sun was now past midday, and he needed to hasten on. Were he to continue on the long road around the murky woods, it would be dawn, at best, before he would arrive. The chance of being seen by people who might take word to his overseer was too great. Cover could be had and hours saved by taking the shorter, direct path through The Forest.

So Fahoul turned and faced The Forest. Although he gave no thought to the stories about it, the twisted greyish trees, the deep shadows and echoing, and the mournful cry of birds within it made him uneasy. His eye fell upon the sign with its warning, and his mood shifted quickly to one of disdain for his own fears. "Fables!" he told himself and strode forward into the shadows. Not more than a few steps in, the dry earth gave way to damp, spongy ground. One step sank wetly into the soil, leaving the impression of his foot behind as he moved on. His stride bespoke confidence and security, but his nervous glance betrayed the inner distress that The Forest roused within him.

As the sounds of his passing died away and he moved into the heart of The Forest, mist began to rise from the imprints of his feet. Thin at first, the vapors rose, swirling, thickening, and suspending themselves in the air — taking a shape of their own.

The gloom remained unrelieved, but Fahoul quickly grew accustomed to it; familiarity breeds contempt, and contempt was a very natural state of mind to Fahoul. For all of its forbidding atmosphere, The Forest roused no evidence of fear in Fahoul. Only the grey, gnarled trees moved in The Forest, and despite the cries indicating their presence, not even the birds could be seen. All about him there was nothing other than the rustling trees and dappled pools of a fitful light that had found its way to the floor of The Forest through the thick, almost unbroken, canopy of leaves. In fact it was the dimming of these pools of light that alerted Fahoul to the clouding of the sky above. Fearing the approach of a storm, he trudged doggedly ahead lest ill weather find him short of his destination. Step upon step upon....

Fahoul halted, catching his breath. He heard a cry like that of an animal, distant and wavering. Had it been the wind? He decided it must have been so and pressed onward. He had traveled only scarce minutes further when he heard it again. The hair on his neck bristled. The sound was clearer this time, and it was not the wind!

Half bestial howl and half something...something that had a human quality to it. The sound was clearer this time; the sound was nearer this time.

Fahoul quickened his pace. His mind feverishly figured that he could barely be to the heart of The Forest if he had, indeed, been going in a straight line, for the clouds had made determining his direction impossible. The howl sounded again, still closer. It was unmistakably coming in his direction. Something in his heart told him what his mind would not accept; it was on his trail. He broke into a jogging run, stumbling now and again in the boggy turf. Again it sounded! This time the sound took on the quality of a demon scream. Panic seized Fahoul, and his pace gave way to a full, frenzied run.

Through the trees and thickets he plunged, branches and twigs slashing at him. He fell to the ground and hurled himself back to his feet. The howl came on stronger now, and it was plain that his pursuer was both tracking him and gaining ground. Fahoul's breath labored, his lungs strained to bursting, and his muscles began to burn from overwork. Now and again the bloodcurdling howl lent wings to his feet, but his body was not the equal to outdistance what pursued him. The wind grew colder and whined about him.

Suddenly the trees dropped away. For a brief moment he thought he had reached their far edge, but before he could even slacken his pace, Fahoul realized he was in a steep gully with walls of sheer rock. Trapped! Frantically, he threw himself, clawing at the gully's far wall, the top just out of his reach. The howl again! This time but mere steps away from him!

Ashen, Fahoul whipped around, his back pressed to the rock. No breath could he take, no sound could he utter save for a strangled gasping as he faced the thing that hounded him.

The being that stood before Fahoul in a half-crouch was his very own image. But what an image! Talons hung from the beast's fingers, and fangs stuck out from the drawn lips. Evil and

murderous intention twisted the creature's entire face. Indeed, to the fevered mind of wide-eyed Fahoul, the beast's face looked like a horrid mockery of his *own* face. Breath rasped harshly past the beast's jagged ridge of teeth, and the glittering eyes bore a look of satisfied, savage triumph.

The two remained, frozen before each other. The minutes turned into ages while a chilling mist began to fall. The beast laughed. The laughter was slow, deep, and dripping with grotesque gloating. The laughter ceased as quickly as it had begun, leaving behind an even more terrifying silence. Fahoul felt his heart would burst at any moment.

Then with a voice that was as much a mockery of Fahoul's voice as was its face, the thing spoke: "Astonished, Fahoul? Terrified of what you see? Sickened? You ought to be! You did not heed the warning, and now here you are. Here in The Forest of the Soul's Mirror, where the real self rises to face any who enter here. Do I disgust you? I ought to! For I, Fahoul, *I* am your real self. All of your greed, your cruelty, your unfeeling treachery, accuse you now in me. I, *I* am your self-seeking animal brutality, Fahoul! I exist because *you* exist! I am the sum total of the sins of your life and the crimes that you have visited upon innocent, undeserving others. You loved only riches and power, and behold! Here is that love enfleshed before you! Everything that you truly are, Fahoul, I am. Without pity or mercy, I am self-serving and ruthless. All this I am because such is what you are. By coming into The Forest, you called me into life, Fahoul, life with but two purposes: to first show your real self to you...and then to bring judgment upon you."

With a disgusting noise that passed for laughter, the thing moved closer. Feebly, the quaking Fahoul begged, pleaded, offered riches, promised reform, but the creature remained unmoved. With a lightning-quick movement, the razor talons lashed out and raked Fahoul's flesh....

❄ ❄ ❄

Fahoul awoke with a scream. Instantly his hands flashed to his aching head. His eyes scanned crazily about for the beast. Slowly, what had happened dawned upon Fahoul. He sat at the edge of The Forest again, exactly where he had entered it. Toward the west the sun lowered itself behind the mountains. Much of the afternoon had passed.

The beast had been nothing more than a dream, yet Fahoul could not make himself move toward the woods. He was thinking — thinking long and hard about what the thing in his nightmare had said to him. He knew there was a message for him in all of this, for there is always some grain of truth to any dream, and to this one he was certain there was more than a grain. No, he would not dare The Forest to prove that it was only a dream. Not yet.

Fahoul stood up gingerly, for his head still ached and throbbed. He decided to let his suspicion of the overseer prove itself with time. There would be no confrontation this day. He turned his back upon The Forest and began walking up the road in the direction of the canyon. It would be dark soon, and he did not wish to be too near The Forest. Besides, he needed to retrace more than his steps, and there was no time like the present to decide how to do that. There were many things that could not be undone, but he knew the whereabouts of his cousin's children, and their price was certainly not beyond him. He could undo much in setting their lives back in order. It was a step. And, perhaps at some time in the future, he could come back to The Forest and not be afraid to face what he might find there.

———————◆———————

"I'm not sure I care for this story so much," said the pilgrim. Although it was too dark to see, Gershom could hear the scowl of disapproval in the pilgrim's voice.

"Why not?" asked the monk.

"Fahoul was utterly evil, without a single good quality. He deserved to die. It's a shame that the creature was just a dream."

"Are you so sure it wasn't real?" The monk's words hung in the silence.

"What do you mean?" the pilgrim asked after several long moments.

"I mean," the monk resumed with careful words, "that the dream was real enough to make Fahoul repent and change his life. Does this not please God? After all, remember that God does not delight in the death of the sinful but in their repentance." Gershom paused long enough to let the words sink in before continuing. "Which makes for greater glory to God? One more death in the world or a life that is turned back to the cause of good?"

"I see your point," the pilgrim grudgingly conceded. "But I don't see how this story has any particular bearing on faith."

"Oh don't you now?" The monk's voice carried more than a touch of irony. "All right, how about this? Fahoul had faith that his dream was a warning — a warning from God to reform his life. And then there's God's faith in Fahoul."

"*God's* faith in him?" This was almost too much for the pilgrim.

"Exactly," said the monk, unperturbed. "God knew Fahoul well enough to have faith that he'd reform. The same faith, I daresay, that moves God to not give up on *you*."

Gershom scored a direct hit. The residual silence told the monk he had stung the pilgrim's conscience. "At any rate," Gershom continued, "faith doesn't always make rational sense. Indeed, it more often than not doesn't make *any* rational sense. It is reliance on things that the world says can't be. For example, and I think this will make my point clearer, there is the tale about Olu of the Yorubas, a man whose whole life is an illustration of my point....

III.

OLU OF
THE YORUBAS

EEP in the bush of West Africa lived a band of Yoruba people on the shores of the Ogun River. Their many years of wandering long behind them, they had settled here for some time and become a solid, industrious community of farmers, fisher-folk, and workers in all manner of trades. And among them was born a male child, the son of Dende, to whom was given the name Olu.

Olu was a handsome and jolly child who laughed and smiled a great deal. These fine qualities made him an easy favorite with people, for the least jest was heartily appreciated by Olu, and he had a way of bringing a smile into the most serious situation. He grew up a popular youth, but it must be said in honesty that not all of Olu's popularity was due to these noble characteristics.

His promising life had been marred by another trait, one that blighted all that he did. This flaw erased any chance of Olu's ever being regarded as a threat to or by anyone in a competitive way and, therefore, made everyone comfortable in his presence. Who, after all, makes a person feel more comfortable than one who is no challenge?

Early on, Olu would (as children do) attempt things beyond the strength or skill of a child. One day, for example, he tried to shoot an arrow for the very first time, having seen an older brother do so. On his first several attempts the arrow scarcely left the bow and fell heavily to the earth. This was not satisfactory. So Olu put all of the weight in his small body into the effort, pointed his aim skyward, and launched his arrow. Oh how it flew! It arched up, up, and higher still into the blue sky where it peaked, hung still for a breathless moment, and fell point-first back toward the ground on the far side of some low cocoa trees.

A scream shredded the air.

The arrow had embedded itself in a sack of yams an arm's length from his sister, who had been milking a goat. Her frightened shriek brought the family running from everywhere. A thing like archery was not taken lightly by Olu's family, and despite the fact that no real harm had been done, Olu was severely scolded, all taking their turns with this youngest member of the household.

The finishing blow came from his father, Dende.

"Above all," Dende concluded, yelling loudly and waving an insistent finger in the poor boy's face, "you must not toy with such things! They are dangerous, and you are too young for skill enough to handle them! Leave them alone, Olu, until you learn to do such things properly! It is not safe because *you cannot do that*!"

Dende turned on his heel and walked away angrily, leaving the small Olu with tears welling up in his eyes. To make matters worse, Olu's brothers and sisters made fun of him for days. But much longer than that did Dende's stinging words echo in the boy's mind.

This was the beginning of those trying childhood days when Olu wanted desperately to help and learn, but all he did — or all anyone *thought* he did — was get in the way.

"Get away from the forge, Olu. You cannot be of any help here. And watch out! You might burn yourself."

"Go play, Olu. You are too young to help with the milking."

"No, you cannot help with the harvest. You cannot handle a

machete yet and might cut yourself. Go back to the hut, Olu. You are only in the way out here."

His puzzled family wondered, as Olu grew toward manhood, why in such a skilled family this boy, alone, was not any good at archery, the art of the smith, milking, or the harvest. In fact he always seemed to bungle a job. Lovable child though he was, still the fact remained: "There isn't much that Olu can do well."

What they meant was, he could not do anything well at all.

But this, coupled with Olu's pleasing way with people, made him all the more popular. After all, Olu could not do anything better than anyone else, and he and the whole village knew it. So everyone felt superior to Olu. Being around him was an instant lift to anyone's self-esteem…except Olu's. As he grew toward adulthood, some began to wonder whatever would he do to earn his living. But they did not wonder long, dismissing the subject by telling themselves that some family members would let him live in their homes doing menial jobs. To their way of thinking, Olu fulfilled a much more important function in the village than the performance of work. "Every village needs a village fool," one young wag declared, "and Olu can be ours, right, Olu?" And everyone laughed as did Olu in his good-natured way, but no one knew or even guessed that tears of pain and humiliation tore at Olu's heart when he was alone.

The most bitter torment to live with, though, was the one that he hid from the sharpest of all eyes — his love for Ilé. Ilé! The very name was magic, for she had been named for the goddess who was Mother of the Earth. The multicolored beads studding her tightly braided hair made all the more lovely this daughter of a river fisherman. Lovely, sweet, kind, and thoughtful, Ilé was loved by everyone, and so (without hope) did Olu love her. Many handsome young men sought Ilé's hand, handsome young men who knew skills and had futures. Olu brought out Ilé's sparkling laugh and even if she did speak to Olu in the marketplace, he thought it was too much to hope that she could care for him. After all, he was a failure. Everyone knew that. He could trust his secret with no one, not even his family, for he could just hear them saying, "Oh, Olu, you can't be *serious!*" or, worse, he feared they would laugh at him.

And so despair haunted his waking moments.

🚀

It was nearing the end of the rainy season in Yorubaland. The high palm trees glittered with moisture and framed green valleys spangled with color, as well as the ribbon of the greenish-blue Ogun River lazily meandering through the land. Here and there on its surface moved a handful of small boats for fishing, the trade of some of the Yorubas in these parts. Daughter of these good people that she was, Ilé was among them. While yet a girl, her father had taught her how to handle a boat. In an old one that came to her family from a departed uncle, Ilé floated down the beautiful river. On this day the spray shimmered on her chocolate-colored skin, her face upturned to the sky.

It was the first good day for boating on the river after too many days of steady rain or too swift a current. In her eagerness, Ilé had not noticed how rotted some of the boat's hull had become during the rainy season. Slowly at first, then with gathering speed, water began to seep into the boat, dampening her feet. Realizing her situation, Ilé turned the boat and headed for the shore. Still some distance from shore, Ilé knew the boat was going to founder, and being a good swimmer, she prepared to leave the boat. As she crouched to dive overboard, a sudden rush in the current threw her off-balance, and with a loud crack her head struck the side of the boat. Unconscious, she fell with her head and arm dangling over the side of the boat, her delicate fingers dragging in the cool water.

A small band of people happened to be on the shore and witnessed Ilé's plight. But swimming was not a common skill and was nearly limited to the fisher-folk; therefore, none of the people on the shore knew how to swim out to save her. Although Ilé was not far from shore, they were helpless to save her as she floated by slowly. All they could do was shriek and wail.

It was their cries that brought Olu, who had been walking and lost in thought in the nearby woods, to the shore. Their clamor brought him running to the river's edge. Olu could no more swim than those already there — years before he had been advised that he would never learn how. The sight of Ilé in the sinking boat and the knowledge of her situation sent him into shock. He knew at the moment nothing, save Ilé, saw nothing but Ilé alone, and had no thought for anyone else than Ilé as he trotted along the shore with the others. Love welled up within Olu, and finally he moved his steps blindly forward toward the water. He seemed unaware of his own movement. Each step brought him closer to the water's edge. A small wave broke on the shore as he put his foot out, and to the astonishment of those there, he walked out upon the surface of the river, striding across the current to the foundering boat! Reaching it, he lifted the unconscious maiden tenderly in his arms and carried her back to the shore as the boat slid beneath the water's surface.

In later years, indeed to his very death, Olu could never remember doing this incredible feat.

Some minutes later, Ilé opened her eyes as she lay on a mat in her family's hut. Her head ached. Blinking, she saw forms all around her, but all were foggy. As the fog cleared she beheld familiar faces, but the nearest one was the first she could identify. She found herself gazing into the relieved face and earnest, round eyes of Olu. He held her hand warmly in his. And as his eyes spoke, Ilé in reply smiled her answer.

Would it astonish any to learn that she wed Olu? Olu, with his earnest eyes and clumsy, appealing ways? She, too, had long been waiting for some sign of love from the likable young man, and she had been perilously close to never seeing it! And would it be astonishing to hear that from that remarkable day forward, Olu's

life turned around? Ilé's grateful father taught Olu the trade of the fisher-folk, not to mention how to swim! To everyone's great amazement, Olu was not only good at swimming, he excelled. Many would be the fine days that he and Ilé would share working on the river, and many more there were with their children. He was even chosen to be one of the village elders. Olu and Ilé lived many happy days, and their descendants are yet found on the land that borders the Ogun River.

"Don't tell me, I'll tell you this time," the pilgrim began. The night was warm, and in the aftermath of this story the pilgrim felt happy and confident. Even the stars seemed brighter. "I believe you're going to tell me that I think too much, right?" the pilgrim told Gershom.

The monk laughed heartily. "Exactly!" he began. "Faith is not having certain knowledge, it is having a *belief* in things that may not make 'sense' but which we know to be true or real anyway."

"So I can walk on water like Olu, huh?" the pilgrim chuckled.

"Oh, no, you'd sink like a stone," the monk returned matter-of-factly. The pilgrim felt a trifle offended by Gershom's blunt honesty. "You haven't learned to suspend your rational mind and just believe, Pilgrim. And in our world of today, that isn't easy. We are all bombarded with 'realism,' and the cost to us is that we rarely have the ability to experience the miraculous. But it can be done."

"Could something that wonderful happen to me if I could learn how?" The pilgrim's voice was rich with a poignant wistfulness.

"Yes, it could," the monk spoke with equal earnestness. "And that is exactly why I chose to share this particular story with you. You see, the awkward place that modern humanity is in lies in that we want to believe, desperately, but our 'good sense' that our society so carefully teaches us denies us the possibility. Life is ripe with possibility, Pilgrim." After a moment he added, "Remember that Jesus told his disciples that if they had faith so small as a mustard seed — which is terribly tiny — they could make mountains move."

"I'd settle for a small hill, Gershom," the pilgrim replied.

"Then believe, Pilgrim, and it shall be yours," the monk answered.

They sat awhile in silence as both thought. The pilgrim asked, "Does faith always pay off that way? I mean, with making everything all right and undoing wrong?" The question was a bit naive, but he asked it honestly.

In the dark the monk smiled sadly. "No, but it can help make sense out of even the worst of things. Consider the following matter...." And he began another tale.

IV.

THE

EAGLET

IGH in a remote mountain range a crag jutted from the sheer face of rock that was the side of a deep canyon. Far below, a mighty, swift river roared between the dark pines on its way to the sea. But from the high crag the river was but a glistening silver thread and its roar a mere whisper, soothing to the ear. A turn in the wall protected the crag from the worst of winds and, in its slight outward lean, gave shelter from most storms.

It was here the eagle had built her nest. She had built the heavy, rugged nest in the early months of spring, and it was here that she had laid the single egg, her first. Through the long days of the nesting season she patiently guarded the forming life within the shell. Day followed day as she anticipated the joy and fulfillment to be had in her soon-to-be-born young one. Now and again she would sense a stirring within the shell and, craning her neck closely, would call softly, lovingly.

And then the day came. Around dawn a first hairline crack appeared in the egg, followed by a dislodged chip. By midday the wet fledgling was out. The mother preened him and provided shelter for him with her great wings stretched out as a canopy. She sent a great joyous cry echoing off the mountain, and it carried far down the length of the canyon. This day her firstborn had come into the world.

The warm summer days swam past. For the mother these were spent in a ceaseless round of hunting to feed her young. Swift and merciless as the huntress must have seemed, she descended with deadly force upon hapless mice or squirrels, yet was gentle and doting with her young one.

The fledgling grew steadily. The mother taught him in the haunting tongue of the eagles. She imparted the eagle wisdom of generations to the restless nest-bound eaglet. The fledgling learned from her about the fish that leaped in the river below, about which animals to hunt, about how to read the face of the sky. But of all his mother said, the eaglet most closely listened to her describe the shifting currents of air and how to ride them, soaring, as only eagles can do. He listened, enraptured, and dreamed of the day when he, too, would ride the wind. On that day the wind itself would be his only teacher, for there is the learning that all creatures must master and which no words can tell.

Each day he watched his mother take flight with great powerful flaps of her wide wings. With what seemed like no further effort, she would then catch the wind and soar swiftly away. Landings, turns…he eagerly watched them all as the mounting urge to fly welled up within his growing body.

Autumn came earlier to the mountain heights as it tends to do. It had put its first chill in the morning when the time had come. For days the eaglet had beaten his strong young wings with the urgency of knowing the time was at hand. At times he half-lifted himself. As he greeted the rays of the rising dawn with a piercing cry of joy saluting the day, his mother knew the nest could hold him no longer.

Mother and son stood abreast at the edge of the crag. The canyon floor lay dark and distant far below, but the breeze and the sapphire sky overhead beckoned.

"Remember," the mother bird urgently reminded in her whistling, clicking tongue, "if you lose control, just hold your wings out tightly. The wind won't let you fall. Then flap with all of your might! Persistence is what gains success."

Nevertheless, as he poised on the brink she watched her firstborn with grave concern. Had she taught him all he needed to know? Was there anything she had forgotten? If he panicked at this height…oh, why hadn't she nested lower! A hundred demons of doubt goaded the mother bird at this moment, but with a push of his legs her son was off, dipping below the brink and then disappearing.

The seconds seemed like years until the mother bird shrilled in delight: He rose! Yards out over the open canyon, his great young wings pumped. For a brief moment he tumbled but quickly went into a glide. With his balance regained, he resumed his skyward climb.

Flight! How small the world he knew from the nest now seemed! It all opened beneath him, revealing many things his mother had told him but until now had remained unseen. Ice-capped peaks, sparkling lakes, other pine-darkened canyons — a host of wonders revealed themselves to his keen eyes. The young eagle felt giddy with the sheer newness of it all. He soared higher still, drinking in the marvels that each widening circle showed him. All this was his! He felt like the very role of king of the birds was now his for the asking. But of all he saw beneath him, nothing was so wonderful as the freedom of the sky itself. His senses drank in its vastness, laced with occasional clouds. He caught a new current that lofted him higher and higher, sending the wind whistling through his pinions. But he did not hear a whistling that moved within the wind until the last second.

The arrow buried itself in the young eagle's side, piercing his mighty heart. The powerful broad wings crumpled, and the great bird tumbled from the sky to the ground, far, far below.

The broken body lay on the valley floor, the fatal shaft sticking out from it. A hunter emerged from the cover of the woods and strode over to where he saw the fatally wounded eagle fall. The man's thoughts focused on what he would do with his prize as he reached the body, for the eagle would bring a good price.

But it was a trophy he would never claim. With a piercing, chilling scream, the mother eagle was on him! Crazed with grief, she hurtled upon the hunter with the full force of a rage that is solely born of heartbreak. While her great wings pummeled him, her talons raked at his face. He made a futile swing with his bow to fend her off, but the iron beak of the powerful bird splintered it. Tearing free, he ran for the safety of the trees. He regained his cover beneath the branches that turned the mother bird back, but not before the furious eagle left long wounds, the white scars of which he would wear for life on his back. Hunters know that the memory of eagles is long; he never returned to the place, being quite content to have escaped with his life.

A knotty stump stood over the fallen bird. The mother alighted there, watching in vain for a sign of life. None came. She hung her head, uttering soft piteous cries, and grieved to the depth of her heart. For three days and nights she perched over her slain young. Waiting. Waiting for what she did not know, but still she waited.

A fingernail moon arose the third night, its thin light making the mountain night seem somehow even colder. With ruffled wings folded around her, the mother eagle watched the wind stir the feathers on her son's body. Again she hoped it was a sign of life. But it never was. The wind rose stronger and colder and began a soft howl, as though the very air mourned with her.

But what was that? A sound, soft and uncertain, caught her attention. She called to her young one, but there was no answer. Then the sound came again! Within the moan of the wind, her

offspring's voice spoke, soft, but clear: "Do not grieve, Mother," the voice said. "You did all you could. The fault is not yours. My life passes on now but, Mother, you taught me to do what I had to do. You showed me how to fulfill my destiny. Eagles are born to fly. And I flew, Mother, I flew. My life was not in vain, and your effort was not wasted. I flew! I flew! I flew...." And the voice trailed away into the wind.

For a long while the great bird perched there in the dark, no longer watching the body below but the stars above. The pain in her heart had lessened, and she felt a strange consolation. Nothing could or would erase the memory of her firstborn, but she could live with that memory now.

As dawn neared, she lifted her great wings, gilded with the rising sun, and flew away. She soared on unseen currents, a sadder but wiser creature who would teach many young fledglings to be eagles and to fly.

In the velvet night, the pilgrim's eyes burned.

"Did this answer your question about whether faith always pays off, Pilgrim?" Gershom asked quietly.

"Yes," came the slow answer. "And I see why you told me this one. There are so many things in the world that make no sense. Things that are pure disaster with no rhyme or reason to them. I would guess that you are telling me that faith sometimes has no answers but trusts that behind the seemingly meaningless events of life, there may be some triumph or purpose after all."

Gershom smiled. The pilgrim was bright and learned quickly. The eyes of his understanding were opening. "And to that I might add that death comes to all mortal things under the sun, to some later than others and to some too soon. Whatever the timing may be, it is the time ordained by forces we do not fully understand. Not that such knowledge makes it any easier to bear and not that the One chooses such painful partings for any of us. They are often chance and accident. But what *is* important and of supreme value is what this tale does teach us."

"What is that?" The pilgrim cocked his head with uncertainty.

"What did the mother bird learn?" Gershom returned.

The pilgrim thought for a moment. "That there really is no death," he answered softly.

"Exactly," the monk replied. "What we call death is not that at all, it is merely change. Life goes on. Your senses cannot prove that to you, Pilgrim. Only faith can."

The pilgrim felt his sorrow lift. "Why, put that way, the story isn't so sad after all."

"I had hoped you might think so," the monk said with a chuckle. "And a good deal more survives the change than ourselves alone. The more we gain here in the way of perfection, the more we take with us, although I caution you that none of us leaves here as a perfected being! But it is amazing how much impact one solitary person can have on all of that. May I share with you a story to make my point?"

The pilgrim laughed. "After all of this, how can I say 'no' now? Please! Do proceed!"

V.

THAÏX
THE DRAGON

HAÏX looked much like what people would expect a dragon to look like...sort of like a cross between a snake and an alligator with plated golden scales on his undersides and glossy dark-green scales above. To top it off he had great leathery wings and bright red eyes. Anyone daring to look at Thaïx had to admit he was a beautiful and graceful creature. He did not breathe fire as legends would have us believe, nor was he as huge as many tales tell us dragons are. From tip of snout to end of tail, Thaïx was barely ten feet long, although that was quite large enough as far as anyone who might stumble upon him would be concerned.

But such a one would really have no cause for fear because — also contrary to the tales — Thaïx was thoroughly gentle and inoffensive. Oh, it was true enough that many dragons were fierce, short-tempered creatures who had earned their nasty reputations. Such ones, however, had gone seeking trouble. It simply was not fair to generalize the horrid behavior of a few to all members of the dragon species.

Thaïx had never gone beyond the familiar peaks and valleys of the mountains in central China. He lived high above the edge of the parched Gobi Desert in the days before the Great Wall had reached the region. Thaïx had been content to remain among his kind — far from the lowlands where humans lived — and content to hear travelers' tales that helped him grow in the ancient wisdom of the dragons.

Thaïx learned from his elders the deep understanding of the world, including many secret things that made him grow very wise indeed. But as the long centuries of the era of the dragons unfolded, Thaïx found his kind to be rapidly declining. The ancients were passing from life, and humans constantly exterminated the havoc-wreaking hotheads. Dragons had never been numerous to begin with, and now the humans were as beyond counting as the stars. Indeed, although dragons were becoming quite scarce in the remote mountains, at the same time humans were settling in large numbers on the eastern slopes. It was humanity's nearness that aroused Thaïx's curiosity about them. Because he was old (even for a dragon) and long past timid prudence, he left his mountain home and sought people in the valley of the rolling Yellow River.

Thaïx alighted near the edge of a forest. A road emerged from it and beside the road was a large rock. He hid behind the rock, thinking it could give him the tactical advantage of surprise to begin a conversation before a traveler might take fright. Thaïx knew only too well the opinions that humans had about his kind due to the unfortunate behavior of a few. He waited, practicing a host of charming little civilities with which to introduce himself. It was not long before a merchant burdened with a large pack came his way.

"Good morning, sir," the dragon began with a well-managed nod. "My name is Thaïx and I have come to...."

"Uhhhhh-WAAAIIII! Dragon! Fierce, horrible dragon!" the man repeatedly shrieked and fled down the road, scattering goods from his pack as he ran.

This was not an encouraging start. But Thaïx, reminded of the unsavory reputation that dragons had earned, understood the man's reaction. Thaïx resolved to try another approach. He made his way down an adjoining path to the wide river and spied a woman washing clothes. Hoping not to alarm her, he quietly slipped up to her from behind.

"A fair morning to you, good woman. Might a weary traveler enjoy the pleasure of your compa...."

"Eeeee-YAAAHH!" The woman screamed, the hair rising on her neck and her eyes bulging out. She flung a wet shirt into Thaïx's face and dove into the river. The Yellow River was swift and cold at this point and time of year, but the woman flailed her way to the opposite shore so swiftly that had there been an Olympics that year, she would surely have won a medal.

Thaïx was discouraged and downhearted. Obviously the element of surprise was too overpowering. He decided to use a more direct approach, allowing the other to see him first. Thaïx hoped this would result in less hysterical behavior. He returned to where the road left the woods again but now sat far enough away to be seen clearly from either direction down the road.

It wasn't more than a few minutes before a small group emerged from the forest but stopped abruptly when they sighted the dragon. Despite all his civilities and protestations of having nothing but the most noble of intentions, they showered him with rocks and fled, shrieking into the safety of the trees.

"Oh, it's no use," Thaïx moaned despairingly. "They are all so terrified of dragons that no one will talk to me."

"I would be willing to," said the voice coming from behind him.

Thaïx turned and found himself facing a slightly built young woman of medium height with a smiling (although *somewhat* apprehensive) face. She leaned on a cane. Thaïx noted that her right leg was bent and that it could not support her weight. But her handicap did not bother Thaïx. It wasn't of any importance in light of the fact that the woman was willing to talk to him. After all, what defect can blemish friendship? Thaïx beamed in greeting. "I am very pleased to meet you. I am known as Thaïx."

"The pleasure is mine," the young woman said, bowing with difficulty. "My name is Mei-Lin."

The two spent some time conversing and getting acquainted by the road until the group last frightened by Thaïx reappeared. They were with more people now and carried clubs and rocks. They were from the same village as Mei-Lin, and when they saw she was with Thaïx, they began to call her "traitor" and "dragon-lover" and other rude names while throwing rocks at both of them. When one struck poor Mei-Lin — who could neither run nor defend herself — Thaïx sprang forward toward the group, roaring with terrifying ferocity. They quickly decided they had better places to be and departed.

But the damage was done regarding Mei-Lin: She would now be an outcast from her people, since the villagers had seen her with Thaïx. The people of the village would not even listen to her. As it was, though, Mei-Lin really had no desire to return and live among fearful people who would not try to understand. Thaïx meant to take care of her now and persuaded Mei-Lin to return with him to his faraway mountains to the west. In a cave overlooking one of the new towns recently settled there, Thaïx and Mei-Lin made a home, sharing the things each knew and becoming fast friends.

It was not long before rumor spread of the wise woman who lived in the mountain cave. She had to be a wise woman, for all very wise people lived in caves, as everyone knew. People began to seek Mei-Lin for advice and learning. Thaïx, who stayed carefully out of sight in the cave, would give Mei-Lin answers from his great supply of dragon wisdom and learning, then Mei-Lin would return with it to the people. To all appearances Mei-Lin merely seemed to withdraw for meditation or to consult some holy book before returning to give people their answers. The people never ceased to be amazed at the wise things that she told them. In return they gratefully gave food and small comforts in exchange for Mei-Lin's wisdom. This eased life considerably for Mei-Lin and Thaïx. Many years passed happily.

Mei-Lin had been a young woman when she first met Thaïx, but now the long white braid of her hair reached her knees. Eventually, as is true for all creatures, the long life of her great friend reached its end. Thaïx passed on, his massive head cradled in the lap of his loving friend who wept bitterly as she watched the red glow fade from his eyes. Sometimes, when an especially wise dragon with an unusually great soul dies, his spirit becomes a new star in the night sky over where he passed away. That night a very bright, glittering star gleamed above the foothills, one with a reddish cast, and people began calling it the Dragon Star. They had no idea how very right the name was.

But poor Mei-Lin! She was outcast by her people back home, old, and now without her best friend. Worst of all, it had been Thaïx, in truth, who had supplied her with all of the wise answers. What would Mei-Lin do without him? Her whole livelihood depended on being able to answer the visitors' questions.

But the most wonderful thing happened. The people kept coming to Mei-Lin, and Mei-Lin found that she had gathered her own store of wisdom, just as Thaïx had. And the people kept seeking out Mei-Lin the Wise for solutions to their problems. They remained just as amazed at and grateful for her answers as ever. In the evenings she would sit and watch the Dragon Star dance above the peaks, and she remembered her old friend. Many years had passed since she had reached out in friendship to the creature feared and shunned by all. She missed Thaïx, but just look at how rich her life was for merely having known him! Mei-Lin marveled at the kindness of fate that had brought them together. They would meet again, she knew. Beyond the peaks above her, she would find her friend again when it was time. But for now she had the light of the star and the light of understanding as reminders of her friend. And Mei-Lin was happy.

Some years after Thaïx's passing, the Dragon Star glowed especially bright one evening. It was low and red on the eastern

horizon. Suddenly a second star, golden and equally bright, appeared so close to it that the rays of the two stars seemed to mingle and shine as one. And with the passing of Mei-Lin the two friends were together once more. And the stars glittered and sparkled merrily.

———————————◆———————————

The pilgrim began speaking, "And the point is that it is good to have faith in a friend even when others disapprove. That was almost too easy, Monk." The pilgrim had found the story to be happier than the previous one but apparently didn't find its message too moving.

"And are you quite certain that there is no further meaning to be found in the tale, Pilgrim?" A taunt seemed to fill Gershom's tone.

"Hmmm," the pilgrim mused. "If there weren't, you wouldn't be goading me like this." He thought for a while as Gershom inwardly thrilled at what a quick learner the pilgrim was proving to be. The younger man lifted his head as a thought struck him.

"Faith in herself," the pilgrim said, half in thought. "Mei-Lin learned wisdom and faith in herself." His tone grew excited. "She was disabled and probably depended on others throughout much of her life. Then Thaïx came along, and Mei-Lin took a chance on a friendship that others would never accept. She became wise and able to take care of herself. Even when Thaïx died, she wasn't destroyed. She had learned many things and to have faith in what she could do!"

"Bravo, Pilgrim!" the monk said. "All of us need to know that we are special — created unique. And whatever gifts have or have not been given to us, it does not change that we are here to share our gifts with one another. There is no one among us who does not have value if we have faith in ourselves and the One who created us as we are."

"But, Gershom," the pilgrim asked, "what if our faith in ourselves isn't returned by others? I mean, what if no one is willing to accept our gift and what we are? Doesn't that sort of undo what you've just shown me?"

"I don't believe or feel so," he replied immediately. "And if you can stay awake for yet another one, I think I know another tale that will show what I mean better than I can say it...."

VI.

JUDGMENT DAY

HE village of Macas nestled in a place blessed by God, nature, and humanity alike. In this sheltered valley of the Andes stood the midpoint of a winding pass that connected the narrow coastal plain of the West with the tropical lowlands of the East. A steady flow of commerce moved in both directions, showering the village with the blessings of prosperity. The weather was reasonable, the scenery splendid, and the living good. The villagers feared God, lived clean, and worked hard, giving thanks for the richness of their lives. The years had bred deep-seated values and decency into the people, who were of one mind on most things and united in the cause of their mutual benefit.

Unfortunately, the villagers were also of one mind toward anything unusual or different. Their memories of bad incidents with travelers dated back generations, thus keeping the people of Macas distantly polite and separate from visitors. The villagers were at least tolerant: After all, strangers always moved on. And what choice was there for a traveler? Macas was the only place of rest and supply along the entire pass. But the Macasians had quite a different attitude toward their own people who did not fit neatly into the community. Slackers, dreamers, those who sought out the company of travelers or who held opinions different from the accepted ones of the majority usually left or were forced out. As is often the case with people who become turned in upon themselves, the people of Macas had become narrow-minded and bigoted.

It was into this very place that Rafael was born. The only child of a couple well into midlife, he was his parents' joy. In the small village church the shoemaker and his wife returned thanks each day for God's blessing of this child. At first the villagers shared in the parents' joy over their long-awaited son. After all, the shoemaker and his wife were pillars of the community, respected and well-liked. With such fine people for parents, little Rafael was scheduled to grow up as a credit to the values of his community, as he fit in nicely and quietly.

But the child was barely a year old when strange deformities began to build upon his shoulder blades. This baffled the village doctor who pronounced that nothing he knew could keep the child from becoming a hunchback. Nevertheless, he gave the worried parents the name of a good doctor in one of the seacoast towns. When good weather for travel returned, the small family made the long difficult journey to the coast. The people of Macas dutifully offered up novenas back home for the success of the family's trip and for good news, for no one wanted such a tragedy in their happy village.

Weeks passed and the shoemaker's family returned to Macas. No, the doctor was quite right, nothing could be done. Yes, the sea coast doctor did have an idea of what the matter was, but Rafael's parents did not want to talk about it. No, they would not keep little Rafael sheltered from the rest of the world. He was their son, and flawed or not, they loved him. God had been good enough to bless them with a child, and they would not reject this gracious gift.

The villagers henceforth considered the shoemaker and his wife to be noble for the way they endured this misfortune so bravely. After all, it took great strength of character to accept the burden that this child would likely become. All of that was understandable and praiseworthy. What the people could not quite grasp was how Rafael's parents not only continued to *thank* God at daily Mass but also did so with double their former devotion, speaking openly of their "blessing." Some thought the shoemaker and his wife were obviously candidates for sainthood, while others dismissed them as being a little "off" from their disappointment and grief.

The years passed and Rafael grew. They were not easy years. He was often the target of teasing, and few children would play with him because of his deformed body. Parents of the few who would play with Rafael tolerated it out of consideration to his parents. But none of the people welcomed Rafael into their homes unless he was accompanied by one or the other of his parents. (It would have been a breach of good manners and hospitality to do otherwise.) But if Rafael or his parents ever noticed how badly the people of Macas treated them, they never gave the least sign of it. The three went on as if there were nothing the least bit unusual within their household. Indeed, they were model citizens and neighbors in their free hours, which made a few feel as though they were trying to put on holier-than-thou airs.

Were his deformity not enough to set him apart, Rafael looked different in other ways too. While he shared the skin coloration and the features of the Latino people in his village, his hair was wavy and sandy — almost blond, not at all like the black straight hair of his own people. Among an almost universally dark-eyed people, Rafael instead had dark, green eyes shot with flecks of gold that caught the sunlight with a metallic glint. The effect was anything but sinister, but Rafael's eyes had a disturbing look to the villagers, nonetheless. To gaze into the eyes of Rafael was to feel guilt before the look of his forgiving kindness — an otherworldly quality that no one could manage to name. Indeed, there was nothing threatening about the boy at all. He was small and slight with a delicate, almost pretty, set of features. Everything about Rafael had an airy effect — everything except his deformity.

In truth, even the deformity didn't burden him much. He had no difficulty moving or any lack of energy. Indeed, his bearing was perfectly normal and erect; it was only the growth that made him seem hunched over. By his twelfth year the boy's growth had become a huge twin-ridged hump on his back as large as his entire torso. His mother made large, loose-fitting shirts to try to cover it, but to no avail. The worst part, which could send a shudder of revulsion through any villager, was when one or the other of the ridges would twitch, as if possessed of an independent life. Indeed, "possessed" was becoming a common way to speak of young Rafael.

By now, none of the children were allowed to play with Rafael at all, yet the villagers still held their real thoughts about the boy to themselves out of respect to the worthy shoemaker and his wife. Rafael's parents astonished the whole village by continuing to give thanks at the little church every day, their faces illuminated with deep joy. It was quite beyond understanding. Perhaps, some said, God gave them the grace to deal with their pain. Perhaps, still others said, they had lost touch with reality and sought to lose their grief in religious devotion. Seemingly unaware of the dark looks that followed them everywhere, the little family went about their business, and the father even began to teach his son the shoemaker's trade. All the while, superstitious fear simmered. The shoemaker and his wife, of course, could not shelter young Rafael forever. They had both been in their middle years when Rafael was born and grew into old age as Rafael entered manhood.

During the winter of Rafael's eighteenth year, the old shoemaker died. The following spring his wife died too. Alone, Rafael continued in the trade his father had taught him. But although he did quality work, his business was not as brisk as his father's. Many townspeople avoided any dealing with Rafael, and some went so far as to send to the coast for shoes. No one socialized with him. Even at Mass, Rafael stood alone in the back of the church to avoid the people's dark looks and movement away from him. The growth was larger than ever now. It arched over his head like a balcony, but both Rafael and it had stopped growing. Some whispered that beneath the shapeless shirt a demon clung to his back. Old women advised pregnant women to shun looking at Rafael, lest their children be born with his deformity. Indeed, people avoided crossing his path for fear of bad luck. In guarded tones people attributed their losses and misfortunes to Rafael. One day a village man who had teased Rafael as a child fell to his death while climbing a mountainside. Despite the time between the two events, people pointed to it as proof that to mock Rafael was to ask for certain death. Whenever the growth on his back twitched or trembled, people crossed themselves and muttered prayers or even curses. Slowly the smoldering embers of prejudice were fanned into the open flame of hatred.

❋ ❋ ❋

The crisis came on a summer's morning — a bright day too beautiful for the events it would see. As Rafael walked past a tethered wagon full of melons, a poorly tied rope gave way. The wagon reeled down the street and crashed into a wall, leaving its contents scattered all over the ground. Cursing, the wagon's owner confronted Rafael, screaming about how Rafael's "witchcraft" had caused the accident. A crowd began to gather, and they nodded their agreement with the wagon man. Rafael meekly took the unfair abuse; it would have done no good to protest innocence to the angry man. Before long the crowd became a surly mob. People's voices chimed in with one-word accusations and epithets like "freak" and "demon."

"Run him out of town!" one voice loudly demanded. Like hypnotized parrots the mob began to echo those same words over and over. "Yes! Run him out of here! Run him out of town! Run him out of town!"

Before he had time to comprehend what was happening, Rafael found himself in the middle of a surging mob. People shoved him roughly and jabbed him with sticks. Ominously, some even began to gather stones as they moved.

At the place where the western edge of the valley met the pass, the land dropped steeply away. The mountains' tall peaks stood like jagged teeth for a backdrop. It was here that the people of Macas pushed Rafael toward the descending trail, accompanying him with cheers and cries of "Good riddance!" He turned and tried to protest against this treatment. Never had his slender body looked so frail, nor had the weight of his growth looked so heavy. For a moment the crowd grew silent, perhaps finally moved to sympathy by the young man's pleas.

Suddenly the great hunch twitched as the poor shoemaker's defense became animated. The great hump rose, shivered, and resettled. A murmur of disgust swept the crowd. Someone shouted, "Kill him!" and a rock sailed through the air, striking poor Rafael on the chest. He staggered backward, lost his footing, and slipped off the edge of the road down a steep incline. The crowd surged to the brink as he fell.

But scarcely had he slipped when the great hunch began to heave and strain. As the mob reached the edge, the heaving shape burst his shirt asunder, and two broad snowy wings spread into the air. Checking his fall, Rafael rose into the sky, circled, and looped above the astonished people. Then with a cry of exultation, Rafael soared away, lost in the sun and the distance. He was never seen again.

Among the crowd at the valley's edge an eerie silence reigned, broken only by bursts of weeping.

❊ ❊ ❊

Some years later a traveler named Miguel passed through the village of Macas. It had been many years since Miguel's last visit, and his memory of the icy, unfriendly village still remained vivid in his mind. To his surprise the people whom he met this time were very cordial. One man from whom Miguel bought provisions even went so far as to invite the traveler to join his family for dinner. The visitor found himself accepting the invitation out of sheer astonishment. And Miguel hadn't been overcharged for anything either!

After the dinner, when the children had been put to bed, Miguel and his host sat alone outside the house watching the evening sky. Unable to contain himself any longer, Miguel commented at great length on what a marvelous and complete change he had found in the village since his last visit. "Was I wrong in my evaluation of your village on my first journey?" Miguel asked.

"No, my friend, you were not wrong," the villager said slowly. "We were very much like that. We thought we knew all the answers. We thought that our obligation to our neighbor stopped with those whom we chose to call our neighbors. We were very wrong. We had so very much to learn." A long, uncomfortable silence followed the host's comment.

"What was it?" Miguel finally insisted. "What changed all of you so?"

The villager looked at Miguel and smiled a bit sadly. "My friend," the villager said, "you would not believe me if I told you." His eyes shone with an odd light as he told Miguel, "Let's just say that God sent us a messenger to show us the error of our ways."

The pilgrim was quite puzzled by this one. "But how did faith triumph here?" he asked Gershom. "I mean, Rafael was run off! You can hardly say that makes for a happy ending, now can you?"

"No. In the sense of having the story end the way we might like to see it end, no." Gershom spoke slowly and thoughtfully. "But if we look at the end result, was not the village itself brought back from its small-mindedness?"

"Well, yes, but....Oh! Now I think I see! Because of Rafael, *their* faith was reawakened, and it allowed them to change themselves. If it hadn't been for him, their story would have ended unhappily. They would never have had their consciences stung, and that's what really made them correct the wicked things they did to others."

"Well said, Pilgrim!" Gershom joined in. "Their faith was awakened not only by an awareness of who Rafael was but also by the example that they saw him set for them in his life of gentleness. This is the same thing that caused former enemies of Christ to believe in him after having denied and rejected him."

"Yes, I can see that. Still..." and the pilgrim's voice took on a sad tone, "I would have liked to know what became of Rafael."

"Of course you would. That is human nature to want to know the ending to every story. We don't like mysteries or unsolved problems, as a rule. But in this life we are presented with many of them. Some things, and the results of some things we do, just aren't meant to be known in this world but *will* be revealed later. For example, consider this next story as a case in point...."

VII.

THE SINS
OF THE FATHERS

N a land to the north of L'Chabra-dìa was a wild but fair country of mountains and foothills clothed in pine. The land stood remote and sheltered, hence, it was little troubled by the outside world. Its people were a gentle, peaceful folk. For many years a good and noble family had ruled over those people. Their walled township was both the only city and the heart of the realm in this region.

In this time before the world forgot its closeness to creation and the air was pure and clear, one of the ruling dukes died and was succeeded by his only son. The young man proved to be haughty and ambitious and shared none of the kindliness of his forebears. He desired the splendid luxuries of the great cities to the south and bent his will toward making the people produce the goods he would need to barter with other lands. Soon the land groaned beneath his oppression, and the gentle people slowly began to grumble against the duke's tyranny and the evil days that his reign had brought.

The duke, however, cared little for what his people thought or felt and only pressed them harder. If they did not do as he wished, he would punish them by seizing their crops, cattle, and humble craft goods, justifying his behavior as being within his rights as lord of the land. Gradually, he fell into the same way of thinking about people, assuming that it was his right to seize any *person* he had a mind to seize. It was in such a frame of mind that he dallied the day when a woman entered his life.

One day as the duke traveled back to his fortified capital, he saw her. She was a simple peasant, yet no lovelier woman lived in his realm. With raven hair, warm chestnut eyes, and a face that was innocence itself, young Marie became the object of the duke's desire. As with all things he felt to be his, he wanted this "possession" too. With no further thought, he commanded one of his footmen to seize the fair Marie and carry her back to his fortress. There he kept her, despite the outraged protests of her horrified kinfolk (who were quickly silenced by the threat of losing what little they owned).

The duke denied the woman nothing but two things she desired most: her freedom and the name of "wife." Despite her shame and captivity, however, Marie remained kind and loving, true to her nature, and in due course of time even the hardhearted duke began to soften. He became considerate and even gentle with her, and her hope grew that one day he would marry her and end her shame. So it was at the end of three years that Marie was overjoyed to find she was with child.

Now that I am giving him an heir, she thought, *he will respect me and make me his wife.* And her hope flamed bright at the thought.

But instead the wicked duke greeted her news icily. Indeed, he saw her less and less as the time for the birth of their child drew near. When Marie did see him, he was either remote or became short-tempered with her. So it was, and time passed until, in the late winter, the woman bore a son...but his father was nowhere to be found.

Some days passed, and then came the word that shattered Marie's hopes like the stroke of a hammer upon crystal: He had just returned from an adjoining realm. There he was betrothed to the daughter of a wealthy nobleman, and they would be wed in mid-summer. When more days passed and the duke had still not sent for her, Marie took their baby in her arms and presented herself at the duke's chambers, wearing determination like a cloak.

What heart could have remained unmoved as Marie pleaded for herself and her child as tears streamed down her face? The duke looked upon her and thought that Marie's beauty did indeed far surpass that of the nobleman's pale daughter. But the thought of his prospective father-in-law's wealth hardened the duke's dark heart to flint. With frozen disdain he told Marie she would be cared for…as one of the new duchess' maidservants. Unspoken was the even greater shame that implied.

Horror filled Marie's eyes. "No! No! You cannot subject me to such shame! I…I thought you cared for me — that our child would be your heir!"

The duke scornfully replied, "No child of a peasant woman will ever rule the land of my fathers. Care? Does a peasant wench like you dare to think that one of my class would actually stoop to loving a commoner?" And he laughed.

Shame and anger struggled within Marie, raising tears that blind-ed and choked her so that she could not speak. Suddenly words did issue from her, but they were in a voice not her own. They were heavy with tones of anger mingled with majesty: "Cruel, proud lord! Unworthy son of a worthy family! Of all your crimes, this one is the worst and has sealed your fate! By a hand of vengeance that you yourself have created shall you fall, for evil rewards itself! You shall.…"

The duke interrupted her speech with a powerful strike of his hand, halting her words and knocking her and their son to the floor. The baby screamed with terror. Marie lay there, amazed at the words that were not hers but came from her own lips. She wondered if she were mad. The duke stood over her, enraged and trembling,

but not so much from anger as from a cold dagger of fear that pierced his soul.

"Your filthy brat of a son," he rasped through dry lips, "will be given to the stablemaster and will be his to deal with. This misbegotten thing you would have rule will clean stables all his days. And as for you," and the dagger of fear pierced deeper, "you will be taken from here, far from here, and will be granted your wish. You shall be married…to the first low-born wretch who will have someone like you to wed! Rejoice!" He turned away and strode from the room.

The next day she rode away with one of the duke's servants, weeping bitterly for the child who had been taken from her the night before. They rode for several days — far outside the duke's domain — before the servant approached a peddler and asked if he were looking for a wife.

"What is the matter with her?" asked the peddler suspiciously. "No one gives something of value for nothing. No. She must have some great fault."

So they traveled on until they met a farmer. "No, indeed," he said. "She has no dowry to bring to my house. And besides," he added, "I want no tainted woman whom another has rejected." And the woman wept silently in shame, knowing now that people would judge her for a sin that was not her own.

They rode for yet another day until, at midday, they met a herdsman. He was a simple and kind man. When the duke's servant offered Marie in marriage, the herdsman looked upon the lovely face, lovely despite her tears and grief, and was moved not only by her beauty but also by his compassion for her sorrow as well.

The servant rode back to the duke's walled town while, before a gathering of relations and neighbors, the herdsman and Marie pledged their vows of marriage to each other. He took her into his home, and love grew between them. Rarely did their rustic home know an unhappy day, and as the years passed, they were blessed with children. Many more years drifted by until Marie passed from this life, happy and surrounded by those she loved. Friends and relatives mourned the loss of Marie and her gentle ways. But in all those years she had never forgotten the first son she had borne and often wondered what had become of her child....

※ ※ ※

Twenty years had come and gone since the fateful confrontation between the duke and Marie. Ten years had passed since the boy, apprenticed to the coarse stablemaster, had run away, driven by the man's brutality. All he ever knew of the duke had been taunts and contemptuous glances. The duke also made certain that the boy knew he was his son in order to sharpen the sting of his disdain for the boy. The knowledge that the duke was his father gnawed at the boy like a cancer. Of his mother he knew nothing, thanks to the duke's keeping that information from him. When the boy ran away, the duke had been glad to be rid of the child whose brooding eyes brought back the stabbing dagger of fear.

But now the duke wished he had every hand that had ever labored for him, for the people of his land had finally revolted. Years of oppression and abuse had made the countryfolk rebel at last, and their pitchforks and scythes ringed his walls.

The duke considered this dilemma in his chambers. The passing years and his thoughtless cruelty were now etched in his once-handsome face. To those wrinkles and lines were added tense ridges of anxiety. The pale wife had died the winter before, but she had borne a son — a pale child who was too much like his mother for the duke's liking. But the baby's presence allowed the duke to still claim his father-in-law's aid. The duke concluded his thinking with a plan: He would try to reach the borders of his land but would leave the baby behind. This would ensure that he could reach his father-in-law, who would send soldiers to help the duke regain control of the situation. *Then*, the duke thought, *I can repay these filthy peasants*. His sunken eyes glowed with a wolflike savagery at the thought.

Just before daybreak the duke sent a group of horsemen out the gates to distract and occupy the peasants. The riders suddenly burst from the gates that just as suddenly snapped shut behind them. The horsemen did not expect this. They did not know the gates would open only once more — to let the duke out. The duke slipped out the gates as the horsemen fought the peasants who greatly outnumbered them. Disguised as a peasant himself, the duke slipped away into the dark, leaving his horsemen to be cut down and killed as they shouted in desparation for the gatekeeper to allow them back into the fortress.

Taking a path into the deep pines, the duke hastened toward the border. The path was one that people seldom used anymore. It twisted and turned around the backs of the mountains, and even if his town were to fall now, he knew he was safely away. Whatever happened, he knew his victory was assured.

In the late afternoon the duke made his way down the far side of the first mountain. There had been no pursuit, but he hastened on, eager for the vengeance he yearned to taste. At the bottom of the valley lay a rushing stream, swollen with the snowmelt. It roared before him as he stepped onto the rough footbridge. He was halfway across, gingerly balancing, when the figure of a young man appeared at the opposite end.

Startled, the duke found himself looking into a bearded face framed by shaggy hair. It was a face that looked much like his own had appeared many years ago. Yet despite the changes of the years, the son who had fled into the hills recognized the duke, his father, and smiled grimly.

Lured by this ideal opportunity for revenge (and the bag of money on the duke's belt), the young man sprang forward onto the bridge, with a spear in hand. The duke could not go back the way from which he came, and here, at this bridge, was the only place that the rushing stream could be safely crossed. No words were spoken. None were needed. The two stood silently for what seemed an eternity until the duke suddenly drew his sword and slashed at the guardian of the bridge. The duke struck swiftly, but his son parried with the spear. Slash! Thrust! And again! The experienced duke had the edge of skill, but strength was on the side of the young robber, strength and hatred. The dagger of fear made it hard for the duke to concentrate. When he looked into his opponent's eyes, he recalled the similar look in the eyes of the young knave's mother who had been banished years before. In that unguarded moment the spear found its place between the duke's ribs.

Clutching the spear, the duke stumbled, lost his footing, and then tumbled into the roaring, frigid waters. Carried for several yards, he then wedged between two boulders where, screaming, he drowned in the freezing torrent.

When the final echoes of the duke's cries had been swallowed in the roar of the waters, the young man stood for a pensive moment, nodded in grim satisfaction, picked up the duke's sword, and disappeared into the pines.

A woodsman found the body some days later and hastened to town with the news. A peace was effected and the new young duke, capably advised, grew up to be a kindly ruler completely unlike his father. So the land once again returned to happier days.

But high in a mountain valley, the bones of the evil duke still lay where he had fallen. The glistening white stones of the stream turned dark where the bones lay. Some say the stones had been stained by the evil of his soul.

The bridge has fallen into disuse. Travelers no longer come that way, for legend has it that near nightfall you can often hear a cold, quavering moan rising from the chilly waters around the darkened rocks. And from the breeze among the pines a whispering voice seems to answer, over and over, "Evil rewards itself. Evil rewards itself!"

"Now," the pilgrim began with a highly cautious tone in his voice, "I can see how justice was done here in the end, but how did this prove to be of any consolation to Marie? I mean, she never knew that the duke got his well-deserved end, nor did she ever know what became of her child."

"She never received any consolation about the matters at all…at least not here," Gershom replied calmly.

Somewhere in the dark the pilgrim emitted a low groan of frustrated displeasure.

"Now, now," Gershom chortled, "I told you that the point of the story was that there are some things which we simply do not know the outcome to in this life. If you'll notice, the woman did, indeed, wonder what had happened to her child. But she lost little thought on useless matters of revenge against the duke; she simply refused to be paralyzed by the injustice that had been dealt to her. She was far too wise a person for that and decidedly too loving."

"Yes, but she surely must have wanted to know that the duke got what was coming to him!"

"You forget, Pilgrim," came the kind but firm reply, "that she once loved him, and a person like her could never give vent to a useless emotion like hate. As Saint Paul wrote in his great tribute to the virtue of love: Love does not brood over injuries, does not delight in wrongdoings, but rejoices in the truth. Truth is not served in the need for revenge, Pilgrim. And it is the mind attuned to faith that can let go of the need for revenge and trust that all will work out as the Creator intended it to. Faith lets go of the need to know and simply trusts."

The pilgrim thought about Gershom's point for a moment and

then said, "You know, I do believe I see what you're saying. But it's awfully hard for most people to stay so levelheaded when they're enraged over having been wronged, isn't it?"

"Of course it is," the monk answered. "I never said it was *easy*, but the path to faith lies along the way of learning how to let go of the need to be *sure*."

The pilgrim looked across the dark chasm at the vague outline of the great abbey as he began to nod off in the deep of the mountain night. This business of letting go of being sure and just trusting…well, he thought it was like trying to be sure of the existence of Gershom's L'Chabra-dìa. At the thought, the pilgrim suddenly straightened and addressed the monk.

"Gershom, I've been meaning to ask you something. L'Chabra-dìa — is it a real place or did you just.…"

"Now let's not get sidetracked here."

"But I want to *know*!" the pilgrim persisted. "This place that you keep referring to — does it exist or.…"

Gershom cut in again. "Now if we get off on that right at this moment, we'll never get around to the next tale."

"*What* next tale?"

"This one," the monk smoothly replied and launched into it before the flummoxed pilgrim could stop him.

VIII.
THE
VISITOR

HE old woodcutter lived deep in the pine woodlands of the great northern forests. For years he had worked among the tall, dark pines, gruff and independent, yet a good-hearted man. He worked hard from late spring into early autumn to earn the supplies that would see him through the biting arctic winter that kept him isolated from the nearest village for weeks on end. He had grown old at his solitary work and reminded the few people who knew him of a gnarled old fir tree that grew rougher and stronger with its years.

Warm days had given way to deep sparkling blankets of snow for many years now, but the old man still fired up the potbelly stove in his one-room cabin, never complaining about it. The cycle of seasons was an old familiar story, and the old man took comfort in its predictability.

The people of the village had come to know and accept his solitary ways, and although he was seldom seen during the hard winters, they knew he was snug in his well-stocked cabin. Indeed, people hailed his reappearance as one of the first and surest signs of spring. Some of the folks expressed concern as the number of his years mounted. They thought he should move in closer. But the old man would only snort in disgust and complain about feeling cramped around too many people and not wanting the inconvenience of moving. The subject was always dropped. And so it was that he continued to live some leagues away from them when the year of the Great Winter hit.

Winter always came early to the pine country, but this year the snows began to fall weeks ahead of time. The old man, having many years of experience with nature and her ways, knew that he would be in for a long, rough season. He made his way to the village and purchased twice the normal amount of supplies he would need for the months ahead. He then returned to his cabin to chop and pile a huge store of wood. He was barely in time.

The wind out of the polar regions sliced like a razor across the face of the land. Raging blizzards swept upon its heels, and in a matter of days the land was left beneath twice as much snow as normal. It was accompanied by a biting cold that froze even swiftly running water. The villagers, after the first shock, dug out and hastened to one another's aid. Miraculously, all were alive, although given a few more days some might not have fared so well. Teams went to work foraging for wood through the mountains of snow while the women set to work weaving, quilting, and caring for the sick, making the best use of all that they had available. Several weeks had passed before anyone seriously thought about the old woodcutter stranded far out in the pines. During normal winters he might be isolated from them for weeks. But in this terrible weather, who could say? Earnest prayers were offered for his safety, but nothing else could be done.

The snow began to fall again.

❄ ❄ ❄

Five months had passed since the old man had last been to the village. He awoke to a pale light. Puffs of his breath floated like clouds above his face despite the fire that still burned in the stove. Even when stoked up, the stove failed to do more than make the numbing cold endurable. Through a frost-laced windowpane he could see a crystalline blue sky punctuated with the solemn spear-points of the pines. And then there was the snow, everywhere the snow, deep and powdery, glittering like diamond dust. The sky would be clear today, but in this far northern land the pale winter sun rose late, set early, and accomplished little.

For months he'd had to repeatedly dig out the path to his woodpile every time another snowfall came. The snow itself hadn't been so bad, but the biting cold seared his clothes like a living flame and kept him from all thoughts of trying to reach the village. Even if he set out at daybreak, he could never move so swiftly as the flight of the short day, and a night outdoors meant certain death. So he waited in his cabin and stoked the smokey stove. The huge store of wood dwindled slowly, but it was reaching the point where he wondered which would go first: the wood or the snow. Despite his years, the woodcutter was sturdy. But even though he could stand in waist-deep snow and fell the trees, alone he could not manage to retrieve more than the branches, for the snow mired the huge logs where they lay. For many days he had tried to chop more wood, only to retreat to his cabin at nightfall, shivering under his blankets until he would finally fall into a fitful sleep.

He began to resign himself to the prospect that he might not see another spring. *I really should have listened,* he told himself, *to people's pleas to move closer*. Yet he still wanted to cling to his precious peace and quiet. *Better to die with peace,* he thought, *than to live with noise*.

So it had gone for five months, months that wore relentlessly on the old man. This morning, in the predawn light, he didn't need anyone to tell him that the bitter cold had gone even deeper: He knew, he could feel it. *Not even these stout walls could hold it out,* he reflected. *And if it gets that cold again tonight? Or colder?* He tried to block out the thought.

All through the day he huddled close to the stove, wrapped in a thick blanket with a Bible perched delicately on his fingertips. All day he read from it as the pale sun swiftly arced across the sky of frozen blue. And as the shadows began to lengthen, his combined prayer and thought was: *Please, let it be swift — don't let me suffer.*

The icy wind began to whine around the corners of the house. Already the deeper cold crept inward from the walls.

Nothing could have been more unexpected than the brisk knock at the door. The old man leapt to his feet so quickly as to topple his chair with a crash. He stood, blanket wrapped around his still powerful shoulders, blinking in disbelief. Was his mind playing tricks on him? Were hallucinations the first stage in freezing to death?

The knock, light but insistent, came again.

With a trembling hand he snatched the door open. A piercing blast of deadly wind stung his face. The setting sun was painting the snowy landscape in vibrant pinks and oranges, highlighted by the midnight blue of long shadows. There before the woodcutter stood a boy with sandy blond curly hair and huge eyes. He stood there, clad only in a simple tunic and barefoot amid the snow and the life-sapping wind. Aghast, the old man snatched the child inside, slamming the door behind them. The colors faded as the sun sank from sight, dragging the aura of its brilliance with it. One after another, the stars began to creep out.

Within, the old man hustled the boy over to the stove. "Poor lad! You must be nearly frozen! Who...*who* could have left you with no proper clothing? I will warm you some...."

"Thank you, sir," the boy spoke in a steady voice, "but I am not cold."

The old man stared at him in disbelief and then realized that the

bare arms he had been briskly rubbing were not chilled or shivering but were warm — much warmer than his own icy hands. The woodcutter leaned back against his small table in astonishment.

"Boy, who are you?" he asked suspiciously. He was even less sure of the boy's very reality at this moment than he had been of the knock at the door.

The child beamed. "There are many ways to answer that, sir. But if it helps you, you may call me 'Clete.' " The old man thought it was the boy's nickname because it was an odd name for these parts, and it didn't help assure him of the boy's reality at all.

Still, it hurt nothing to talk to him, the woodcutter reasoned. In fact it was sort of nice to have someone to talk to, even if he *was* a phantom!

"Clete, where is your home?"

"Around," said the boy with a general and vague wave of his hand, "not too far, yet far enough." The old man decided that the boy must not know his actual whereabouts, and this detached air was his way of dealing with the panic of being lost.

"What were you doing out here alone?"

"I was sent."

"*Sent!* By whom?"

"My Father."

"Your *Father!*" the old man exploded. "Why did he send you out, unprotected, in this, this...." he began to sputter.

"Oh, he sent me to be with you." The tone of this statement was utterly matter-of-fact, as if this information were perfectly understandable and the occasion of the visit quite normal.

"To be with...me?" the woodcutter said in an almost inaudible voice.

"Yes," the boy chirped with a pixie's grin. "He felt you could use my company tonight."

"He...sent you out...here...in this frozen wasteland...on this bitter night…all to risk death here with me!" The old man was nearly hysterical.

"Not exactly," replied the boy. "I am to keep you company until the morning and then," he brightened, "bring you home to our house."

"Child, you and your Father are mad!" the woodcutter stormed. "I don't know how you survived to get here, but I cannot do the same. I am old and.…"

"You're not so very old," Clete interrupted with a sweet smile. "Anyway, you'll manage with my help." His certainty as he said this had a curiously reassuring effect on the old man.

The woodcutter just sat there, blankly staring at the child. Now he was quite sure that the cold and isolation had finally gotten to him.

The boy merely smiled in return as if his presence there were the most natural and normal thing in the world. "This is a nice little cabin," he remarked, looking about. "How long have you lived here? Did you build it yourself?"

The old man found himself, despite his disbelief, answering the questions. Slowly, the two fell into a steady conversation. The talk went on far into the night. It was good to share companionship again, and the old man laughed and smiled in spite of the noticeable and steady chilling of the room. So engrossed was he that he scarcely paid attention to his trembling or the numbness of his limbs. The boy, however, did not seem cold at all. *Naturally,* the woodsman thought: *Why should a hallucination feel cold?* Still, they went on talking. Just past midnight Clete coaxed the protesting old man into bed and tucked him in firmly. The thick fleecy covers were as good as threadbare, for they did not warm the woodcutter at all. The boy sat on the edge of the bed.

"But you *must* be freezing!" exclaimed the woodsman.

"I'm fine," said the boy, laying a warm, loving hand upon the woodcutter's wrinkled face. The old man was so cold that the boy's touch seemed feverish. "I'll be right here when you awake. Sleep now." The old eyes closed wearily, and he yielded to a deep, peaceful slumber. The hours passed to the pale dawn....

※ ※ ※

The villagers had barely survived the bitter freeze as they spent most of the winter huddling into the better houses to keep warm. But survive they did. The winter winds and cold eventually died down, and a few of the hardier men decided that it was time to learn of the old woodcutter's fate.

The men set out shortly before dawn. They arrived by midafternoon intending to stay overnight at the remote cabin. Beards caked with frost, they entered the cabin, calling loudly and hopefully for the woodcutter. But one man, silent and distracted, remained behind, staring at the snow alongside the small building.

Inside the cabin, everything sparkled from the frost as the late afternoon sun played through the windows. In his bed the old man's body seemed to be coated with diamond dust, appearing to be asleep. But he was not asleep. The men stood with bared heads, silently holding their hats in their hands as they prayed for their distant neighbor who had succumbed to the harsh winter. But upon the old man's face was a sweet expression of peace without the slightest hint of pain. Indeed, the face looked young, so very young. The men stood there just looking at the old woodcutter's body until the man outside called to them with a quavering voice.

The snow was clean and deep, the air still. The man pointed at the snow. There, frozen into the snow's surface, were the bare footprints of a man and a child. Footprints, side by side, that wandered away together off into the pines, into the shadows, to vanish somewhere toward the east and the sunrise.

"What have you learned from that, Pilgrim?" the monk asked softly.

"That we're never really alone," came the confident answer. "That God is always with us and we're never alone."

"That's a statement of faith, you realize."

"Yes, I do. And I never thought I'd ever hear myself saying something like that. But this story makes me feel...hopeful. Confidently hopeful. I don't *know* that death will be like this, but I feel certain that I'm right to trust in my hope."

Gershom smiled in the dark. This was a breakthrough, and the best part was that the pilgrim was discovering all of these things for himself. The monk spoke again: "Very good, Pilgrim. But let me pose a question to you and play the 'devil's advocate,' if you will. This hope of yours is born out of a positive ending to a story that affects each of us in that we all hope *our* lives will also end so happily. But what if you are called to make a sacrifice that is anything but happy? And what if in your making that sacrifice you never know if what you did was the right thing or if your effort was all in vain?"

The pilgrim was silent for a moment. "I do eventually start to learn, Monk," he said wryly. "I guess it is faith that would allow me to take such a risk, right?"

"Precisely!" Gershom affirmed. "And, as it so happens, I have a case in point."

"I felt certain that you did!" the pilgrim said, laughing.

IX.

HANNAH OF SOROKI

OROKI was a relatively peaceful town during the waning years of the Middle Ages. Although a stout wall ringed the town and strong gates guarded its entrance, these fortifications had rarely been needed by these peaceful people who lived above the banks of the blue Dnestr River. The entire land of Moldavia basked in luxuriant peace in those days — a hard thing to hold since it was so perilously fragile. But the times were good and Soroki was enjoying decent prosperity and abundant harvests.

It was not a town that enjoyed lavish excess, nor was it the envy of powerful neighbors. This was a large part of why it enjoyed such peace. But it was a desirable place to live for those who had no liking for the glittery appeal of the great cities. For its people, the modest, clean shops of Soroki and the town's central square were the source of contented pride.

But not all was well in Soroki. There were the usual frictions common to all peoples, though mostly of a nonserious nature. But for some time trouble had been brewing between the followers of the Cross and those who worshiped beneath the Star of David. The former were the majority of Soroki's people, and the presence of their neighbors in the Jewish Quarter caused them constant irritation.

It was not always so. In the early days, despite their differences of belief, the Christians and the Jews got along very well. But among the Christians in these days prevailed an attitude that some occupations (moneylending, for example) were suspect or even totally contrary to the teachings of their Lord. The Christians of Soroki frowned upon any professing believer in Christ who embarked upon such activity for a livelihood. Few Christians cared to call down social censure upon themselves by lending money. But as is often the case with unstated and unclear laws, the need for borrowing money was always there. Since it was not necessarily wicked to *borrow* money, the Christians turned to other parties who could and would lend them the money they needed. So, by default, the Jews took over such activities because they had no reservations about lending to their Gentile neighbors (unless, of course, there was a concern about getting repaid!). So it was that through moneylending and other commercial enterprises many of the Jews grew prosperous.

Unfortunately, the more prosperous the Jews grew, so grew the mountain of Christian resentment toward them. Ever since the days of Jesus, there had been a residue of uneasy suspicion between the two faiths — a suspicion that could turn to hostility. Such was the hostility that had started to fester in Soroki. As the years passed, tension mounted between the two groups, and their differences became steadily more exaggerated. Soon these differences solidified into the stones of a high wall of ill will, and both sides forgot that they worshiped the same God. Despite this and an occasional clash, there was peace in Soroki, a peace as brittle as first ice, but peace nonetheless.

It was into this stage of Soroki's long life that Hannah was born in the Jewish Quarter. A smiling sweet child with huge eyes and a bright laugh, Hannah brought great joy to her parents. Always eager to help and kind to the elderly, she was a favorite everywhere in Soroki. Hannah helped her brothers sell their father's crafted goods in the square where the great church and the smaller synagogue faced each other across the cobblestones.

Nowadays the feeling was that the two buildings stood in a face-off that mirrored the edgy rivalry between their respective peoples. Hannah knew these tensions existed and often felt them there between the two houses of worship. But it was there in the sunlight of the square that she felt closest to God. To Hannah the synagogue and the church were merely mirrors that reflected different facets of the great mystery of God. They were the twin hearts of her town, hearts that used to beat as one.

It made Hannah happy to be there, even on cold, grey wintery days. That happiness spread from her heart to everyone she met, and as the years swept by, she matured from a lovely and charming little girl into a beautiful, intelligent, and enchanting woman. The dark eyes of Hannah moved the hearts of every young man in Soroki. But if she ever favored any one of them, she never let it show. Hannah was in no hurry to marry, to the great frustration of the young men in Soroki. Even the young Gentiles wooed the beautiful maiden in the square, no matter how much their families might frown on their desiring a Jewish girl. Hannah treated these men no better or worse than suitors from among her own people; she was equally sweet and steadfastly frustrating to one and all.

Now Hannah was no flirt, either, for she did not seek these attentions. Her heart waited for a certain man she had yet to meet, but while she waited she could bring herself to be unkind to no one. Rumor had it that her hand was promised to the rabbi's son, but she did not love the young man. Although the prospect of such a match might be thrilling, Hannah's doting father would never make her marry against her will. The rabbi's son called often, and every day at least one bouquet of flowers brightened the small booth in the square.

But things were not always so pleasant.

Sometimes, when tensions were high, gangs would come into the Jewish Quarter and move through the narrow streets shouting ugly slogans, scaring people indoors, and breaking things. Lately there had been more of these provocations. Once Hannah's father returned home bleeding from a cut on his forehead caused by a rock thrown at him. Hannah's brothers voiced angry threats of revenge against their father's attackers; but the father, being a man of peace, gently silenced such talk. So as the days grew shorter, Hannah started taking a roundabout route home to avoid passing a tavern where drunken louts would call out suggestive, demeaning things to her. Their words had brought pain to her heart and tears to her eyes. But she never said a word about her humiliation to her brothers, for her father's peaceful ways were the ways that she wanted to follow.

There had been talk lately of hateful new laws that would restrict the Jews from enjoying the freedoms that were the right of all people in Soroki. Day by day tensions grew. But very suddenly, in the early autumn, all that was forgotten and set aside in the face of a common danger: The Tartars were coming.

The Tartars were a warrior people from faraway central Asia. Late in the previous century they had swept out from distant Samarkand, led by the great warlord, Tamerlane. His armies had rolled across Persia and the Middle East, humbling even the mighty Turks. Now, Tamerlane's armies posed a threat to ancient, venerable Constantinople. With its conquest in mind, Tamerlane had sent part of his army north around the Black Sea under one of his most capable and barbaric lieutenants, Tadzhik. Tadzhik had been with Tamerlane through most of his conquests. He had even had the "honor" of being one of those who helped Tamerlane execute his horrible revenge upon the city of Isfahan for having dared not to open its gates to him. The example of Tamerlane's atrocities there spread fear like a carpet before his hordes everywhere they went. Now the plan was for Tadzhik to create a diversion on the northern front of the Byzantine Empire, which Soroki was a part of. That would force the Empire's troops away from protecting the eastern line of battle. Tamerlane hoped to outflank the Byzantine emperor and crush his forces. All of Moldavia was threatened, and Soroki was right in Tadzhik's path.

✝   ✡

The armies of the duke had assembled some distance east of Soroki. As they awaited the coming of the Tartars, the people of Soroki strengthened their defenses, stockpiled provisions, prayed, and waited for news from the eastern horizon. It was not long in coming.

The rest of the duke's soldiers reached Soroki in full flight, fleeing the overpowering first wave of assault by the fierce Tartars. The duke's armies had collapsed, and what was left of them was now in Soroki. The losses were not overly great, but the duke's army had been forced to leave all its supplies behind. Barely had Soroki's gate shut behind the last retreating refugee when the Tartars appeared on the horizon. They surrounded the walls of Soroki, sized up its defenses, and proceeded to pitch camp all around the town. Now, if the Tartars defeated the duke and his forces, all Moldavia would crumble. Nearly two thousand additional mouths had been added to consume Soroki's supplies, and the Tartars decided to wait. The siege had begun. From the walls of Soroki at night the Tartar campfires seemed to rival the sands of the seashore in number.

Despair set in swiftly for Soroki. The days passed, slowly, one dragging wearily behind another, but Soroki held on, though grimly. However, the added weight of the soldiers they sheltered was draining their provisions rapidly. Before this siege the people of Soroki assumed that if the duke were defeated, Tadzhik's hordes would pass them by for more important places. But Tadzhik would not leave the duke, safe behind Soroki's walls, to gather new troops. Such troops could gather their forces and follow Tadzhik's army, attacking at an inopportune moment. As long as there was such a possibility, there was, for Tadzhik, no place as important as Soroki.

The siege began because of the duke's presence, true. Now, nearly a month later, the Tartars stayed for an additional reason. Never had any city withstood them for this long. Soroki's stubbornness galled the Tartars, and it had become a matter of pride to level it and let Soroki serve as an example to others in this northern land as Isfahan had been an example in faraway Persia.

Inside Soroki, Hannah helped care for the wounded and the dying, fast added to by the daily attacks of the Tartars. They were making good with their efforts too — a section of the wall was beginning to crumble. If that were not enough to worry about, there was more. Hannah's father helped distribute food throughout the town, careful to preserve as much as possible for as long as possible. But he came home one night and grimly told his family that the meager supplies would run out within the week. Even if the wall held, starvation awaited them. Either way, the Tartars had won.

Hannah's mother began to cry. Weary and beaten as he felt, Hannah's father took his wife in his arms and held her gently. But Hannah did not cry. She sat, saying nothing, lost in thought.

The dawn came coldly on the twenty-eighth day of the siege. Its red light played across the walls of Soroki and, in that light, one of Soroki's guards found a rope that had been let down. Looking out across the fields he spied the figure of a woman making her way through the Tartar camp. *Betrayal?* he wondered, *a traitor?* But it could not be, for he was certain that the woman was Hannah! His cries brought many to the wall, and the word rippled through the streets of Soroki.

She had dressed in her finest dress, one put away for the day of her wedding. Despite that intended purpose, she wore it now. Dressed in all her most beautiful things, she was lovelier than ever. The Tartars among whom she passed followed with covetous eyes, but none moved to touch her. They dared not, for although she was beautiful, she had come seeking Tadzhik, and none would risk crossing their murderous leader.

He was not long in coming out to her. Big, dirty, and cruel-looking, Tadzhik's hard face softened at the sight of Hannah. His eyes scanned her approvingly as he made comments to his men. Hannah could not understand his language, but his tone told her all that the words could not. She turned her face to him and beckoned him with her eyes. The look was not lost on Tadzhik. *Obviously, she is a bribe*, he thought, *a beautiful prize to coax me to leave Soroki*. But Tadzhik had no intention of leaving. He would rob and burn the town...and keep the beautiful bribe for as long as she pleased him.

Tadzhik walked over, wrapped an arm about Hannah's waist, and pulled her roughly to him. His men laughed and cheered rudely, and Tadzhik, casting his leering look at his men, laughed too. But as he turned toward Hannah's face, the laughter died on his lips. In Hannah's eyes there was no fear, and although a smile crossed her lips faintly, it was the smile of grim determination. A shock passed through Tadzhik's body as the dagger in Hannah's hand found its place in his cold heart. It was then that he realized this was exactly what she had wanted him to do.

A half-dozen arrows moved like lightning from the bows of Tadzhik's men. The arrows swiftly found their target in Hannah's back. She slumped and fell atop Tadzhik's body. From the walls of Soroki came a cry of anguish from the watching townspeople. Enraged by Hannah's death and shamed by the example of her courage, the duke flung himself from the wall calling for his men...and revenge! The cry was quickly caught up. Axes, pitchforks, butcher knives, *anything* was snatched up throughout Soroki within minutes. With the duke at its head, the army burst forth from the gates. But this time there were not merely the two thousand soldiers of the duke. This time every able-bodied man of Soroki (and even some women!) went with him. More than ten thousand descended on the stunned Tartars. Without Tadzhik they fell into confusion before the unexpected onslaught. The battle raged well past midday, but it ended with the Tartars flying in full rout back toward Samarkand. Half their number lay dead or dying on the banks of the Dnestr. Soroki was saved.

Yes, Soroki was saved, but its rejoicing was short-lived as Hannah's father cradled his daughter's body, carrying it back into the town. Beneath the grey sky he silently brought the body to the square where the people had gathered in celebration. All fell silent when he appeared. With eyes full of tears and a breaking voice, he spoke: "Here is my daughter, my child, my joy! Here is she who gave her life so that all here might live. Here is my daughter, who died for us! My child, my Hannah…." And with that, the old man dropped to his knees, clutching his daughter and weeping bitterly. The grey sky began to drop cold raindrops as, one by one, the people gathered around Hannah and her father. The sky wept. And so did all of Soroki.

The people of Soroki erected a small monument in the square, placing it where Hannah's booth had stood midway between the church and the synagogue. It was here that they both buried and honored her.

Following Hannah's self-sacrifice, many Jews and Christians passed one another at the monument. Occasionally they glanced at Hannah's monument together, exchanged greetings and offered a joint prayer. The Tartars never returned, and on the banks of the blue Dnestr, Soroki lived again in peace for many, many years.

The pilgrim's voice fell with sorrow, but it was not a sorrow brought about by the tale itself: His sorrow stemmed from his own lack. "I wish I could have that kind of courage," he said. "I mean, to be able to die for someone else. But I just can't see myself doing anything like that. Does that mean I'm weak, Gershom?"

"No," the monk replied with warm understanding in his voice. "It merely means you don't take lightly the gift of life that has been given to you. Courage like Hannah's is born out of deep, deep faith that takes a long time to acquire. It doesn't happen overnight, although it may surface very suddenly in the face of a crisis. I don't imagine Hannah herself ever thought about deliberately sacrificing herself to save another until the moment made it necessary. It is the deepest faith of all, Pilgrim, to be able to give oneself to save another and to do so with no assurance at all that the sacrifice was successful. But as the Lord said, there is no greater love than to give one's life for a friend or a loved one or even for someone you do not know. The truly heroic persons are not wild adventurers with broadswords or blazing guns, but the ones who can value the gift of life in another more than the gift given to themselves." He paused. "Do you know who Saint Maximilian Kolbe was?"

"Certainly," the pilgrim answered. "He was the priest in the concentration camp who volunteered to take the place of a condemned prisoner so that the prisoner could live."

"Do you think he had any assurance that the man would, in fact, live to survive the concentration camp?"

"No...no, I guess he couldn't possibly have known, could he?" the pilgrim replied slowly and thoughtfully. "Yet he did it anyway. I admire that kind of courage, Gershom. I admire the kind of faith that people like that have. I'd like to have faith like that myself."

The monk spoke solemnly, "Then you shall someday. For desire for any good thing is the first step toward achieving it." He gave the pilgrim a moment for the thought to sink in before he continued. "Faith, like any good thing, is something that you must want if you are to have it. Yet for all of your efforts, faith will still come to you as a gift. A gift is a positive thing if we use it correctly, but we can choose to distort it too. Even faith may be destructive."

"Now wait a moment, how can faith be anything other than good and constructive?" asked the pilgrim.

"Because once the gift of faith is given to us, it is in our hands to use as we wish. Like all gifts, we can misuse it," the monk answered. "If we choose to, we can place our faith in the wrong things and defeat the purpose of the gift. May I clarify what I mean by yet one more tale?"

The pilgrim laughed. "Have I stopped you before?"

"No," the monk returned, also laughing, "you haven't. Yet this needs to be the last one, for the day is coming on and we have spent the entire night in our talks together."

The pilgrim looked eastward and thought he saw the first hint of the dawn. Their conversation had indeed filled the entire night, yet the pilgrim wasn't sleepy at all. He turned back to Gershom and said, "Then let's make the most of the night that remains. One last tale, and we'll call it an end."

The monk smiled at the pilgrim's eagerness and, for the last time, began again....

X.

THE MIGHTY GORM

ORM'S cramped vessel sliced across the vastness of space away from the sun and its vivid bands of color and away from his home world of Xi that orbited it.

Xi! How hatred flared within him at the mere thought of it! How hard he had worked for its ungrateful masses! After all, *he* was the one who had brought peace to Xi by uniting it. True, the war it took to accomplish this had been long and cost both resources and lives, yet the goal had been achieved. All he expected in return was to be its ruler and overlord with the right to determine the lives and livelihoods of its people. How small a thing he had asked in return for the blessings he had bestowed upon Xi. And they *dared* turn upon him!

But that had not been enough of an insult. The people of Xi had given him only two options — imprisonment on Xi for life or exile in space where he *might* find a habitable world. Gorm had built the planet's prisons well, and there was no chance of escaping them. Mighty Gorm therefore chose exile. After all, his luck had never betrayed him before. Destiny had favored Gorm until now, and he remained confident that it would do so again. So here he was, leaving thankless Xi behind. Not forever, he thought. Should fate guide him to an inhabited world, he vowed he would subdue its people and make them serve him.

I am still the Mighty Gorm! he thought. He knew he would one day return to repay his ungrateful people.

Gorm charted his course into the heart of the solar system that the sun orbited, leaving Xi behind. The months of space travel passed slowly. As his vessel passed by one world (a larger one than Xi), his instruments showed it to be a cold, dry planet with no ability to support life as Gorm knew and understood it. Beyond that he came to a double planetary system. One of the worlds was about the size of Xi but again was thoroughly lifeless. However, the instruments on his vessel showed strong promise of life on the second watery planet that orbited with the first.

Gorm sensed that this was his chance. He set his controls and nosed into the heavy atmosphere. The air was thick and murky to his eyes, and even on the daylight side of the planet, it was difficult for Gorm to see. As his sounder warned him about the rapid approach of the planet's surface, Gorm spotted something like a runway and landed his small craft. The energy involved in fighting the gravity and the atmosphere had totally consumed the vessel's fuel. Like it or not, Gorm was marooned.

Upon exiting, Gorm found that his craft was sitting upon an artificial landing place. It was very wide, and although made of a rough, crude material, it gave him positive hope for finding some sort of intelligent life. His luck was still with him! Fate had not abandoned the Mighty Gorm! And Gorm was meant to rule, so the future was now written in stone.

It would be best if the inhabitants were not too advanced, he reasoned. *Then they will be that much easier to subdue*. Rule was his destiny, and it could not be altered. But as Gorm walked along the foggy path, he came to an astonished halt. A huge structure loomed in the haze before him; its sheer mass and height were larger than anything on Xi. *What great luck!* he thought. Obviously, the towering structure of rough reddish blocks must be a place of great importance. Fate may even have led him to their global head-quarters! The runway ended abruptly against a stone platform centered before a curious rectangular insert in the building's face. Its purpose eluded Gorm as he looked up at its sheer face before him. Gorm pressed a bar on his belt and lifted into the air to the top of the platform. His skybelt worked sluggishly in this gravity, and Gorm reflected on how the planet's pull taxed his own strength. The gravity was like stifling heat — oppressive and wearing, but Gorm was abnormally strong and managed to get around despite such obstacles.

There was an opening between the stone platform and the rectangle in the facade. Although he had to stoop over to do so, Gorm entered the structure through this opening. *How crude this entrance is,* he thought. *The ones who use this structure must be very small.*

To Gorm's surprise he found himself wading through head-high stalks of some sort of bunched fibers. Although the fibers appeared to be growing, they actually sprang from a woven mat beneath his feet. Obviously, the mesh was seeded and cultivated by the inhabitants to encourage the fibers' growth for whatever purpose they served. *Clever*, he thought, *but they need better tending. There's some green in them, but they are mostly brown...obviously dying.* Gorm decided it would be best to remain hidden at this point, so he did not use his skybelt. Instead he chose to push his way through the fibers, for they hid him quite well. After all, he knew nothing about this planet's inhabitants yet. He soon thanked the wisdom of that decision.

A faint droning was growing louder nearby. It drew closer and louder until it hurt Gorm's ears. Finally he realized that the source of the sound was somewhere in the air above him. He strained to see through the murky air. A hazy shape came into view.

A fat, misshapen black body hung beneath membranous, vibrating wings — the source of the droning. Huge, faceted eyes dominated the creature's swollen head. The beast swept by overhead, then began circling Gorm. It flew rapidly, and Gorm tried to keep a wary eye on it. Once it almost caught him off-guard as it swept by, its skinny dangling legs dragging the tops of the fibers as Gorm ducked. A disgusting stench followed in its wake, making Gorm nauseous. By this time he had decided this huge thing was unintelligent and that it was trying to make him its prey. Gorm marveled at a race that could coexist with beasts like this, or perhaps this race was not advanced enough to have a choice. They may not have, but Gorm did. Already the thing was back. It flew straight at Gorm, but this time he was ready. He drew his ray gun from a side pocket, and in an instant he zapped the creature, leaving it to drift across the fibrous stalks as lifeless ash.

The danger was past, but Gorm was more on guard now. He feared that where one such thing had been, more could be. Such beasts might even be sentries for the creatures who built the huge building. Gorm resumed pushing his way through the stalks.

The hazy air made visibility poor, and Gorm's straining eyes began to throb. Tall, narrow columns now rose before him, and when he looked up, he could see that they supported something very big. Not seeing any ready purpose for these things, Gorm decided they were some odd sort of monuments. Even his own monuments on Xi were not this grand…if any still stood. *Xi! Just wait, all of you!* his mind raged and seethed as he lusted for revenge. Yes, they would pay! Somehow he, Gorm, was going to become master of this race of great builders and with them would return to inflict his vengeance. *Mighty Gorm*, he vowed, *will do this!* In his mind Gorm began the execution of his enemies by the hundreds, amusing himself to the point of a savage laugh.

But his dark fantasies were soon broken by a new sight. Two long, low masses of soft pink appeared ahead. Gorm figured they were some type of embankments or support structures. Each warm

mass led to an enormous white sphere made of a soft material where each embankment ended on its respective side. The sphere occasionally quivered and pulsed, and soft gurgling sounds flowed from its far side. The soft unfamiliar material sent a thrill of hope through Gorm: Whatever this was, clearly it gave evidence that the inhabitants of this world were advanced beyond a primitive technology.

Gorm picked up his pace through the fibers, moving between the two embankments toward the sphere, indistinct in the thick air. By now excitement was an electricity that coursed through his veins. He had found them! The monumental builders of this world! The sphere, he was sure, held what he sought. *Surely the masters of this place are within this sphere,* he thought. Until now, it seemed that the fibers all around him indicated an agricultural society too primitive to pose any threat to Xi. All the evidence he had seen until now indicated a rather backward pre-mechanical culture that somehow was able to build on a huge scale. Gorm wondered about the purpose of the landing strip where his spacecraft still sat, but then he dismissed it as having some other ceremonial purpose. But *this*, this great sphere pulsed with an energy that made the very surface beneath him tremble. This was not primitive. True, it still left this new world woefully behind Xi's state of advancement, but Gorm knew he could remedy that. His single weapon should prove more than a match for anything they might have developed. He had years of life left, and so Gorm felt sure that he could propel this society ahead in a relatively short time. Then he could finally seek his revenge on Xi.

Gorm had nearly reached the base of the sphere when the surface beneath his feet began to shake violently, throwing him down. As he fell, he glimpsed the pink, fleshy embankments thrusting forward and upward, but the view was cut off by the stalks about him. He lay on the trembling surface and looked up. There above him the white sphere heaved toward the heavens with an unsteady wobbling. Up, up it went, peaked in its motion, and with a movement in Gorm's direction, plummeted downward. Gorm's eyes grew wide at the realization that the sphere was heading straight for him! He fumbled for his weapon but failed to reach it. The shadow of the sphere covered him, and a split second before it crushed him, Gorm let out a high, piercing scream.

❊ ❊ ❊

The man at the table, startled by the sound of a tiny scream, nearly choked on his coffee. "What was that?" he gasped.

"I...I don't know," answered his equally startled young wife. "Why, it sounded like a tiny voice that...." Her eyes shifted to the carpeted floor. "Oh, Jerry, look!" she said with a sudden expression of delight, forgetting the strange sound. He followed her gaze to their chubby grinning baby beaming up at them. "Little Josh has learned to sit up," she gushed happily, "all by himself! What a good baby!"

And the baby smiled even wider.

Peals of laughter echoed down the mountainside. The pilgrim said, "So much for big, important, mighty Gorm!" he laughed again. "Mr. Bigshot...snuffed out by a baby's butt!"

"I'm glad you appreciate the humor, Pilgrim," Gershom interrupted, "but get hold of yourself. It is just before dawn, and the good monks of Montserrat are already stirring. If you keep laughing like this, they'll think a madman is loose on the mountainside!"

The pilgrim marshaled his composure. "You're right," he said, swallowing hard. "But that was delightful! I see what you mean about misplaced faith. Gorm was so out of it that he couldn't even see that he was tiny, instead of the grand master of the universe that he fancied himself to be."

"Many people suffer from that delusion, Pilgrim," said the monk. "And that is a natural result of placing faith in ourselves or things instead of where it belongs — with the One. All faith placed in the Creator is honest, honorable, and proper. The gift must be given back to the Giver — the one from whom it came."

The last stars of night burned brightly in that moment before the sun began to rise. The pilgrim looked up at them thoughtfully for a while, thinking about whether there might be other beings out there contemplating his existence on Earth. A thought brought him back to Gershom with a question. "Gershom, what is the reward of faith?"

"Faith is its own reward, Pilgrim," the monk solemnly responded. "It is its own gratification. That is why even one who may suffer for his or her faith can see that suffering as somehow worth it all. These people know that the sufferings they endure are unimportant. It is *faith* that justifies it all for them."

"I don't quite follow you."

"The truth is simply this: It doesn't make the slightest bit of difference to God whether we achieve anything by our acts of faith. All God asks is that we show faith with our trust and our willingness to open our hearts. When we exercise faith, we empty ourselves and allow God to enter in. It's when we have nothing to offer in-and-of ourselves that God fills our lack and does wonderful things. It is our faith that gives the opportunity."

"I think I see. Why this is the point you've been leading up to all night, isn't it?"

"Yes, Pilgrim, it is. Yet all the tales can do is point out the way to you. To reach the end, *you* have had to do the work and walk the path." Gershom lowered his head in thought for a moment and then raised it again. "Tell me, Pilgrim, what is it, exactly, that you've learned from each of the tales we've shared tonight?"

The pilgrim took a deep breath before beginning. "Well, in the first one, I think it was...." One by one, they reviewed each tale as the pale light began to grow around them.

THE TALE OF
SMALL AND DEEP

(EPILOGUE)

ERSHOM and the pilgrim returned to silence for a while. Across the canyon the morning light gilded the great abbey of Montserrat in gold.

"You are a skillful storyteller, Gershom," said the pilgrim. "I thank you for your stories. To say that I found them fascinating would be an understatement! I can't say they've answered all my questions, but they have given me much to think about."

"That is all they were meant to do, Pilgrim; they cannot answer your questions for you," replied the dark-robed figure. "The tales are but guides to be pondered over. Each one who hears them must decide what their meaning is. There are many more tales, but these particular ones are for you and your needs. Consider them well, Pilgrim, and may they help you find the end of your quest."

The monk paused, looking thoughtful for a moment. Then, with a hint of a knowing smile, Gershom spoke again: "Spring, it is said in L'Chabra-dìa, has many voices, and were we to listen with an alert heart, we might hear something for our own benefit. It was on a fine spring morning that He Who Sleeps Not, listening to the voices of spring, chanced to overhear two particular voices in conversation.

"The first voice was high, soft, and timid, and very much upset. Indeed it carried the quality of tense edginess that goes with desperate determination. The second voice came from the darkness that surrounded the first voice. The second voice was not as fearful as the first but was instead warm, familiar, and reassuring. The second voice was kind, yet carried suggestions of great strength and agelessness. It was very deep, yet He Who Sleeps Not could not identify the voice as either male or female.

"It seems it had become time for Small, the first voice, to leave Deep, the second voice. Small was determined not to go. After all, there was comfort, warmth, and security in Deep's embrace. Why leave that for an unknown future and possible dangers? Before leaving such predictable and familiar safety behind, Small demanded to know what this new future held in store.

"Deep, however, offered no assurances at all, for the future was indeed uncertain. But if Small were ever to achieve a future worth living, a chance would have to be taken. And the decision was Small's to make; neither Deep nor anyone else could or would make that decision. There were no guarantees, only possibilities. 'Life,' Deep said, 'is always a chance; it depends so much on choices and the flow of one's destiny. It is also a gift; someone has to give it for it to be passed on. The giver takes the chance — the giver and no other.' "

Gershom continued, "The choice was Small's, who took a long time in replying. When an answer finally did come, it was an affirming 'yes' that set mysterious forces in motion, forces that began to change Small in that very instant. Feeling the changes, Small became frightened, but Deep calmed Small's fear, for the changes were all a part, a vital part, of Small's new life.

"The last thing Deep said to Small was, 'I'll never be far away. Part of you will always be here with me. I will be supporting you and will always know everything that happens in your life. And I'll be right here waiting, waiting for the day you return.'

"Some time later the flower broke from the rich supporting earth and climbed into the air. It climbed and climbed, unfolded, and in wonder and joy, looked for the first time upon the face of the sun. And all that Small was meant to be, timid Small had become."

Gershom shifted his eyes to the rising sun, now clear of the horizon. "We are like that flower, Pilgrim," he said softly. "We stay in the familiar safety of our lives, fighting the call to grow and change. And we can do so indefinitely if we so wish; no one can force us to choose. The choice is ours. That choice, Pilgrim, is faith. Faith carries no guarantees, no security. But it is the life we live through faith, the chance we take, that makes us all we are meant to be — were *created* to be. There is no fulfillment without it." Gershom smiled at the pilgrim, not out of amusement but in kinship. "You haven't lost your faith, Pilgrim," he said. "Faith waits ahead of you in this very hour. She waits for your choice."

Within himself the pilgrim felt an unfamiliar yet comforting feeling. He looked away from the monk across to the great abbey, ancient and yet forever young in the morning light. Words returned to him: "How very much like L'Chabra-dìa," the pilgrim said, though not without a hint of regret, "for Montserrat is real."

"Do you think L'Chabra-dìa is not real?" the monk asked.

"The stories are but stories, so surely the place itself is a legend too, is it not?"

"Who can say what is real and what is legend?" Gershom's tone was utterly serious. "If, as Christ said, what we think in our hearts is as real as the act, could it not be that what we believe in our hearts is as real as the fact? Ah, but I am talking like a philosopher, and what has philosophy ever proven? No, my friend, it must be as you have said, no doubt. The tales are merely fables. L'Chabra-dìa is, as you say, a legend."

Gershom dropped his gaze for a moment. When he raised his eyes again, the pilgrim went numb, his jaw slack. In Gershom's eyes blazed the light of twin suns! "Or is it?" the monk said.

APPENDIꟾ

Scriptural and Theological Commentaries on the Tales

THE PILGRIM AND THE MONK *(Prologue)*

Although God can be encountered anywhere and at any time, we like to think of meeting holiness in an awe-inspiring setting. For that to happen for our pilgrim, I purposely chose an awe-inspiring setting — the ancient Abbey of Montserrat in Spain, not far from the city of Barcelona. It is a revered place of pilgrimage, so it becomes a natural place for our pilgrim to arrive at. The abbey is built high on the side of a rocky mountain on a shelf of rock overlooking a dramatic drop.

But to make the point of Scripture itself, God is not always to be found in the dramatic. The prophet Elijah found that God's voice spoke to him, not out of the wonders of nature but in the quiet of a stillness that followed all of the wonders that he witnessed (1 Kings 19:1-12). In a similar way our pilgrim finds what he seeks (although he does not know it at the time) not in the great shrine itself but in the open air, under the night sky surrounded by stars and led by the quiet voice of the monk, Gershom. Gershom himself is symbolic, for the name means "foreigner" and is taken from the name given to the son of Moses (see Exodus 2:21, 22). We are all "foreigners" or "strangers" if you will, and so it is that this monk, who is a passing pilgrim himself, becomes a teacher of our pilgrim. In monastic tradition monks for centuries have had spiritual masters or guides, so in this monastic setting it becomes appropriate to give one to our pilgrim on his journey in search of faith, a faith we all seek, and therefore, we can all identify with his quest.

Tale I. TURN AND PERDIR

The surface symbolism for this tale is rather obvious, at least in the names of the central characters. "Turn" speaks for itself, for he was a converted person, the entire idea of conversion being a turning toward God. "Perdir" is a name I took from a Spanish verb for "to lose." It is in these names and the characters that they represent that the story-within-the-story is found.

The Bonding bears a very deliberate sacramental flavor, and it is, for the purposes of this story, a representation of the Sacrament of Confirmation. The parallels are obvious: Both are community celebrations, both are rites of full initiation, and both are consciously chosen by the person receiving the rite. I made a deliberate point of having Perdir's family take a hands-off attitude instead of trying to pressure him into accepting The Bonding because, like Confirmation, it is not a thing that can be forced upon an unwilling party. Oh, a person can be *made* to "accept" Confirmation, but usually only on the surface. The real conversion that Confirmation signifies is valid only if it is a real accepting and choosing on the part of the person receiving it. The sacrament is the bestowal of the Holy Spirit, the same as in the apostolic era (see Acts 8:14-17), and it is the sealing of the believer into full fellowship with God. That's not to be taken lightly. In the Bible, Simon the Magician had the wrong attitude toward the power of this sacrament, and we only need to look at Peter's response to see how wrong Simon was (see Acts 8:18-24). The power found in the Sacrament of Confirmation is the same power that descended upon the apostles at Pentecost — a power so startling in its effect that it led to the conversion of three thousand witnesses (see Acts 2:1-2)! But these people made *conscious, deliberate* choices to convert; they asked Peter what they had to do to be saved too, and his response was that they were to repent and *turn away from* their sins and *turn to* the person of Christ. Then, he said, they would receive the gift of the Holy Spirit (see Acts 2:38-39). Only believers received the gift of the Holy Spirit. It was the final sealing mark of the Christian.

So, do I mean to imply that without the Sacrament of Confirmation (or The Bonding) a person will be lost or will go to hell? No! The failure to receive any sacrament does not, by itself, cause any of us to be lost. The ultimate consideration here is the grace of God in the matter. Perdir was lost because of his overall *attitude*, not just his refusal to participate in The Bonding. The commitment to the values of the Astrakar that went along with The Bonding was something that he didn't want. Such a commitment would have limited Perdir to a lifestyle of charity, honest virtue, and simple living. Confirmation has that same limiting effect on the person who receives it in good faith. See Acts 2:43-47 to discover how the lives of those who received the Holy Spirit were changed.

If we have made honest and true commitments to Christ — the commitment that Confirmation implies — then there *will* be a change in the way we live and act. We will base our lives on the Spirit-centered values Paul wrote about (see Galatians 5:22-26).

Like Perdir, we all have the freedom to reject God's offer of the Spirit. But should we do so, then the consequences are ours to endure. The choice to live life in the Spirit is demanding, but it is also rewarding. Jesus promised us this. All the way back to the days of Adam and Eve, God challenged yet also made promises to the people, but the people were always allowed to choose for themselves whether they would follow or turn away from their Creator (see Deuteronomy 30:15-20). The choice is ours. May it be a choice that leads to life and happiness like Turn's and not the consequences of Perdir's choice.

Tale II. THE FOREST OF THE SOUL'S MIRROR

We *all* know or at least have heard of a person who is a "Fahoul." This is the type of person spoken of in Psalm 52 — a person who depends on personal wealth and the security in being wicked instead of relying on God, who is the shelter of the helpless. Since the Fahouls of the world love wickedness and do hurtful things to the innocent, the writer of the Psalms tells us God will demolish these wicked people forever (see Psalm 52:7). How? By simply letting such people pay the consequences of their own evil actions. Caught in their own traps, they are punished by their own evil and hurt by their own violence, as was Fahoul in his nightmare (see Psalm 7:14-17).

We pay the penalty of our own sinfulness — we and no one else. Each one of us pays the price for our own wrongdoing, although God is only too willing to reward us for repenting and turning back to good, a repentance that was Fahoul's salvation. But "when a righteous man turns away from what is right and does wrong, he shall die for it" (Ezekiel 33:18). This is not God's will but the natural end of doing evil. As Paul put it so bluntly and well, "The wages of sin is death" (Romans 6:23), and the reward of being in union with Christ and doing his will is eternal life. There is no condemnation for those who are in union with Jesus, but for those who choose to let unredeemed human nature control them (like the beast in Fahoul), they become God's enemy. They end up not being able to please God, and their nature ends in death (see Romans 8:6-8). God certainly does not delight in this and didn't send Jesus to condemn the world but to save it. But should we choose to turn toward evil in defiance of God's gracious gifts, we had best be prepared to face the consequences on our own.

In the parable of The Rich Fool, during the very hour that the rich man was busy congratulating himself on being wealthy to the point of being beyond all harm, his soul was in its greatest danger (see Luke 12:13-21).

Rich "Dives" (as tradition has named him) couldn't imagine what he had done to merit hell until informed that it was for nothing he *did* but rather for what he *didn't* do when he was indifferent to poor suffering Lazarus (see Luke 16:19-31). It was not the proud rule-abiding Pharisee who was justified to God in the temple but the repentant tax collector (see Luke 18:9-14).

Perhaps the most pathetic story in the Bible is that of the rich young man who wanted to follow Jesus but went away rather than give up his great wealth to do so (see Luke 18:18-30). Jesus' metaphor about it being harder for a rich man to enter heaven than to squeeze a camel through a needle's eye sums up the danger that riches can pose. This, at the bottom of it all, was Fahoul's real sin; he loved money more than people and God.

"The love of money is the root of all evils" (1 Timothy 6:10). It leads people away from God and basic human decency. Notice, please, that it is the *love* of money and not money itself that is the problem! The love of money (which Fahoul definitely had problems with) makes us grasping, hardhearted, and cruel. These are the types of evils that the Psalms frequently speak of and are evils that God loathes. God has warned humanity over and over again about these pitfalls, but now and always, it seems, there will be many who simply choose not to hear the warnings.

In the end we are all visited in some form by our own evil, as was Fahoul. Our loving God does not condemn us in these cases; it is our own actions that condemn us.

If the end of Fahoul's story seems unfair — if you thought he really was rotten and deserved to have his nightmare be real — remember that God does not desire the death of sinners but their salvation. The entire fifteenth chapter of Luke's Gospel contains parables Jesus told about how wonderful it is when those who are "lost" return to God's love and commandments. If God could find enough forgiveness to pardon even the sins of the repentant town of Nineveh (see Jonah 4), let us not play the role of Jonah and insist on a self-righteous demand for "justice" that does not allow God to be all-merciful as we hope that he is!

Tale III. OLU OF THE YORUBAS

Too often words can lead to what is called a *self-fulfilling prophecy*; that is, something that we hear so much that we start to believe it and then live it in our lives. Such was the case with Olu. All he ever heard from his family were harsh words that led him to think of himself as a failure and a clown. It was a short step from that to his actually *becoming* a failure and the village fool: the words of Olu's family became a self-fulfilling prophecy.

These kinds of prophecies can come from ourselves, parents, teachers, friends; even wives and husbands utter them to one another. It is likely that no one means for these ugly prophecies to come true. Certainly, we don't wish them on ourselves. But that doesn't make us any less responsible for them. Jesus condemned the scholars of religious law for burdening people with great weights of commandments but doing nothing to help people bear these burdens (see Luke 11:45-46). These leaders, therefore, were guilty of and responsible for the poor opinion that the people had of themselves. No wonder Jesus stressed the worth of every person so strongly in his preaching to the people. He himself said, "Are not two sparrows sold for a small coin? Yet not one of them falls to the ground without your Father's knowledge. Even all the hairs of your head are counted. So do not be afraid; you are worth more than many sparrows" (Matthew 10:29-31). Jesus told us not to fear the death of the body as much as death of the spirit, which people and their words cannot kill but can grievously wound. Such wounding is a serious sin.

As part of the Sermon on the Mount, Jesus gave us teachings about anger, adultery, and so forth, in which he boldly claimed that to *think* something is the same as doing it. In fact, in the same section of the gospel where he spoke on divorce, he did not blame the divorced wife if she remarried (considered adultery in the eyes of the Law) but on the *man* for putting her in that position (see Luke 5:31-32)! Jesus clearly teaches here that our thoughts can have power and that we can be responsible for the harm that our thoughts or actions may cause another, no matter how "right" we think we are (see Matthew 5:21-37). In other words we tend to act out and become what we think about ourselves, and incorrect thinking leads to bitter mistakes in our lives. The Bible tells us, "Put away from you dishonest talk, deceitful speech put far from you" (Proverbs 4:24). The writer goes on to say that we should never *say* anything that isn't true and should have nothing to do with misleading words or lies. Why? Well, putting the commandment against false witness aside, we should avoid misleading words of all kinds because of the impact they have on *other* people. A kind word can ease a worried heart, and "a harsh word stirs up anger" (Proverbs 15:1). Words have a great deal of power; they can preserve life or destroy it, and the consequences of our words are ours to live with. If our words are misleading and cause someone to lose faith, Jesus has said it would be better for that person to be bound with a heavy millstone and dropped into the sea (see Matthew 18:6, 7)! Words may *never* be taken lightly by the believer. Whoever said, "Sticks and stones may break my bones, but words will never hurt me" was either incredibly tough or didn't realize the damaging power that words really have to wound, and wound deeply.

In the end Olu learned much and prospered by it, but it took an event that undid all the damaging thoughts he had for years taken to heart. It is certainly possible for the wounded heart to heal, but it is better not to wound a heart to begin with. Words, like Olu's arrow, should be handled with caution and carefully aimed.

Tale IV. THE EAGLET

There are tragedies in life that leave us reeling and wondering what on earth is wrong with a world in which good people meet with disasters. Many people question what purpose God has in allowing such things to occur, although people don't usually go to the extreme of blaming God for actual disasters. Wondering why God allows tragedy is quite natural, and God understands; we humans don't like puzzles or stories that end the "wrong" way. Our world is full of such sad and troubling happenings. But the problem is by no means new! People have pondered the riddle of innocent suffering for ages. The biblical Book of Job shows one man's classic attempt to solve the mystery.

But maybe the problem is in the way we look at unfortunate events and our insistence on knowing why they happened at all. In the Book of Wisdom we read that the death of the righteous is not a sad tragedy for them. In fact the death of the righteous is no kind of disaster at all, for they are at peace (see Wisdom 3:2-3). The sufferings they have endured have been minor compared to the blessings in store for them from God, and far from having an ignoble end, they are like the fire-refined beauty and worth of gold in heaven.

We often see people who live close to Christ suffer fates that we think shouldn't happen, while we also see wicked people enjoying the best that life has to offer and meeting no untimely end at all. Psalm 73 addresses just this quandary and reminds us that although the wicked seem to prosper, that is basically an illusion in the here-and-now: The wicked *do* meet a bad end. They will face the punishment they have earned, if not in this life, then in the next. The righteous, on the other hand, are rewarded by God's receiving them with honor. If we believe in the eternal life that Jesus Christ won for us, we must trust that justice wins in the life to come and that God will put things right for each of us.

In the Bible, Judas Maccabee prayed for the souls of those who had fallen in battle fighting to free Judea from Greek oppressors (see 2 Maccabees 12:38-46). He had no doubt that the dead would be raised. If God hears our prayers for the dead, then he is open to intercession for them to ensure their reward. And if a person dies and goes to God to be rewarded, can we really say that person's end was a disaster?

Saint Paul devoted an entire chapter of 1 Corinthians to the subject of the Resurrection, first talking about Christ's rising and then going on to speak about the glories we may expect in our own resurrection (see 1 Corinthians 15). Paul tells us we will be raised immortal and, therefore, perfected. This should not be surprising since Jesus promised that not even so much as a hair on our heads will be lost when God raises and rewards us (see Luke 21:18). Again this is one of those faith issues: We have to trust that God is faithful in his promises to us and can and will do for us what Jesus has said. If a good person meets an unhappy end, that is indeed a tragedy for us but not for that person because the faithful will live with God.

> As an eagle incites its nestlings forth
>   by hovering over its brood,
> So he spread his wings to receive them
>   and bore them up on his pinions.

(Deuteronomy 32:11)

Our consolation is in knowing this truth about God. We can take comfort in being assured that our faithful loved ones are with God and that everything they endured has been made right by the Creator. The Resurrection happened in order to show us that death will lose its power and be destroyed forever, thus leaving us victors in Christ. If we believe that, then we know there really is no death, and people who suffer on earth can find peace and safety with God in the next life. Put into perspective, we can see that no matter what suffering life may hand us, in the bigger picture of God's eternity, all is well.

Tale V. THAÏX THE DRAGON

It is so easy to dismiss a person by going on the fact that he or she may belong to a group we dislike, suspect, or fear. Such was the problem at work in Thaïx's case. Despite the fact that he was perfectly harmless and possessed excellence of character, the vast majority of humanity reacted to him with fear — a fear based on what they had heard about dragons in general. They had no regard for the possibility that Thaïx was *different* from what they had heard was supposed to be true. Only Mei-Lin gave herself the chance to learn differently, and for her trouble she was blessed with deep, true friendship and grew in wisdom through her association with her wise friend. Unfortunately, people tend to be less like Mei-Lin and more like her fearful villagers. Mei-Lin dared to befriend an outcast and was, therefore, rejected for associating with the "wrong kind."

Although few of us will ever befriend a being of a completely different species, we *do* have the opportunity to befriend other people who are also rejected for being "different" and the "wrong kind." Like the people from Mei-Lin's village, we can run the risk of missing out on really worthwhile friendships when we experience petty fear and mistrust.

The Church has a longstanding position against racial discrimination. Such discrimination is basically a form of fear. In the twelfth chapter of the Book of Numbers, Moses' brother and sister criticized him for marrying a Cushite (Ethiopian) woman. Miriam and Aaron, Moses' sister and brother, truly should have known better. They even went so far as to suggest that because of this breach of social custom and marrying the "wrong kind," Moses had lost his claim to being God's chief spokesman. As a result Miriam and Aaron claimed to have authority equal to that of Moses. Eventually, God called them all together and scolded Miriam and Aaron (*not* Moses). God then afflicted Miriam with leprosy until Moses asked that she be healed.

Jesus constantly scandalized his disciples and Jewish society in general by talking to the "wrong kind." He spoke to the Samaritan woman (a definite social no-no, since the Jews and Samaritans were at odds over religion and other matters) and then even converted her and her fellow citizens to the gospel (see John 4:1-42). Jesus also healed a Canaanite woman's daughter whose eloquent plea for help moved him to help this woman who was not of the "lost sheep" (the Jews) to whom he was sent (see Matthew 15:21-28). Out of ten lepers Jesus had healed, the only one to come back and thank him was a Samaritan (see Luke 17:11-19). In the parable of The Good Samaritan, Jesus showed decisively that "our neighbor" is also the person who is supposedly of the "wrong kind" (see Luke 10:25-37).

Jesus often talked about his Father's will and what God wanted people to do in their actions toward other peoples. Jesus knew that the Father had not changed his mind since his revelation to Isaiah:

> I come to gather nations of every language; they shall come and see my glory. I will set a sign among them; from them I will send fugitives to the nations: to Tarshish, Put and Lud, Mosoch, Tubal and Javan, to the distant coastlands that have never heard of my fame, or seen my glory; and they shall proclaim my glory among the nations. They shall bring all your brethren from all the nations as an offering to the LORD...to Jerusalem, my holy mountain.
>
> (Isaiah 66:18-20)

It is no wonder, then, that the risen Christ told his disciples to "Go, therefore, and make disciples of all nations" (Matthew 28:19). That is exactly what they did. We can see this in the story of Philip's preaching to the Ethiopian eunuch without any regard for the fact that the eunuch was a Gentile and a black man (see Acts 8:27-40). Philip knew it was much more important that the eunuch desired baptism in the Holy Spirit.

The Spirit continues to give us the same message today, as do the pope and the bishops of the Church. *All* people are equally precious in God's eyes. Before we judge another based on what we see or what we've heard about "their kind," let's stop and consider whether or not we may be passing up an opportunity to get to know a worthwhile human being who will enrich our lives. It is difficult to be a Mei-Lin who stands up for what is right and refuses to go along with popular opinion. It is even more difficult if we risk being shunned by the people who mean the most to us. But it is the truly Christian thing to do. God wants us to reach out with love to others who are waiting to learn about his love.

Tale VI. JUDGMENT DAY

Everything said in the comments on the tale of *Thaïx the Dragon* apply equally well to the story of Rafael. Again we find people judging based on appearances alone. Even though there is no racial question involved, the judgment of the people against the "deformed" Rafael is just as unfair and just as evil. The real identity of Rafael is an old theme in Scripture: In the Book of Tobit his namesake, Raphael, is an angel sent to help young Tobias during a dangerous journey. It is not until the end of the journey that Raphael reveals himself at the proper moment, and not before. Angels disguised as humans visited Abraham. They also visited Lot in Sodom (see Genesis 19:1-11). It was the threatening behavior of the people of Sodom against Lot's heavenly visitors that moved Lot's guests to strike the crowd outside blind.

There are many other examples, but perhaps the most notable of all is the encounter of the two disciples with the risen Christ on the road to Emmaus. These men didn't recognize Christ for who he was until he revealed himself and then vanished from their midst (see Luke 24:13-35). The Bible contains many such stories of heavenly beings frequently taking on human form in order to teach valuable lessons at various times.

Saint Martin of Tours was once confronted by a beggar, and Martin gave the man half of his cloak to keep him warm. The beggar was then revealed as Christ, a vision that moved Martin to seek Baptism and entry into the religious life. Martin acted out the ideal set forth by Jesus who said, "Amen, I say to you, whatever you did for one of these least brothers of mine, you did for me" (Matthew 25:40). At the same time Jesus also clearly said that when we fail to behave with kindness and decency toward others, we fail him too. The villagers indeed failed in this respect. They failed Rafael, and they failed Christ. Yet they did not *totally* fail because they eventually realized the evil of their ways.

Why did they even fail to begin with? They were, after all, regular (although hypocritical) churchgoers. Certainly they were familiar with the golden rule: "Do to others whatever you would have them do to you" (Matthew 7:12). They had probably heard this passage in the proclamation of the gospel many times.

The problem was that they had not acted on it.

The people of Macas knew all these things, but they had never opened their hearts to them…or to Rafael. The knowledge of his true nature came too late for them, and a golden opportunity was lost. In a very real way the people of Macas were judged, not as severely as a sinful Sodom but in their stung consciences and in their memories of their shameful actions. They were indeed punished. In failing Rafael they had failed the Lord.

We, too, fail the Lord when we are unkind to others. Maybe our unkindness doesn't take the form of racial bigotry but is instead aimed against someone who is disabled, unpopular, socially backward, weak, or even obese. There are so many ways to fail Christ when we fail the people God sends into our lives. Is it possible to avoid this sin altogether? Perhaps, but it would take a superhuman effort and a great deal of God's grace. The best we can do is ask God for the grace to grow in love and kindness toward others and to keep the words of the golden rule ever before us. If we can keep ourselves mindful of that (and believe me, I have to remind myself daily!), we will find our treatment of others changing. The result can be that others change the way they treat us too. That is how true Christian love begins. Jesus Christ touches our lives and we, in turn, reach out and share that touch with others. If we really want the world to change, this is the way to go about helping it do so.

During his ministry, Jesus of Nazareth encountered many "deformed" people: lepers, people with physical disabilities, and people with mental and spiritual illnesses. He reached out with compassion, love, and understanding to these people, and in doing so he healed them. We, as a people of God, are called to do the same. When we encounter a person who may repulse or disturb us, before we act or say anything, we must stop and ask ourselves, "If I were this person, how would *I* want to be treated?" If we take the time and trouble to do this, we may find in that deformed person a Rafael who will reveal the beauty of a hidden nature to us.

Tale VII. THE SINS OF THE FATHERS

The whole point of this story is: God is a God of justice and will deal with the wicked who fail to repent in a way they deserve. God's judgment spoke through the mouth of young Marie, and the knowledge of her sentence being just and deserved put the cold chill of fear in the wicked duke's heart. The son who brought the sentence to pass symbolizes the justice that people's wrongdoing visits upon them. People pay for their own sins, not those of others, and yet they can avoid the penalty if they turn from wrongdoing (see Ezekiel 18:21-24). Revenge is not for the Christian believer but is to be left to God. People must trust God with putting things right in his own time.

The problem of seeking justice in a world that is often unjust and unkind is as old as human history. Surely it would be so much better to follow Christ's commandment: "Love one another. As I have loved you, so you also should love one another. This is how all will know that you are my disciples, if you have love for one another" (John 13:34-35).

We must treat others with the same respect and care we ourselves would like from them or at least refrain from doing the harm to them that we would not wish done to us. Yet one has only to turn to the Psalms to know how often this is not the case. Friends we love and trust may betray us (see Psalm 55). We may find ourselves surrounded by enemies who seek to harm us for no good reason. Such people move us to call upon God to save us and to punish those who have harmed us (see Psalms 17 and 57). But despite our powerful enemies, we can place our trust and confidence in God to set things right (see Psalm 56).

It is not up to us to judge people, for no one but God may judge our brothers and sisters in this world. It is important to remember that "judgment is merciless to one who has not shown mercy; mercy triumphs over judgment" (James 2:13).

There is such a human tendency to want God to "deal out justice" and do it *now* for our enjoyment. It is human to want to see one who has wronged us punished. Another's undoing might be justice, but there is nothing just about wanting to gloat over it. It is enough to know that we may not see the justice of God's ways, which are higher and therefore different from our own, but that there is justice to them, and in the end

God sees to it that right is done (see Isaiah 55:8-9). As God restored all that the righteous Job had lost, he distributes justice to all his creatures, whatever they may deserve (see Job 42:7-17). In the whispers that blew from the pines near where the duke fell, "evil rewards itself." God never unfairly punishes but simply allows people to suffer the consequences of their own sinfulness. If we do not see the justice in the situation or if it is not speedy enough to satisfy us, then we must remember that it is our own human ignorance and not God's wisdom that is at fault.

Stories similar to the duke's have been part of human history over and over again. We cannot keep these things from happening as long as human nature is what it is and as long as people insist on ignoring the golden rule. But we can remember that God, who has all things in hand, is a God of justice who is able to save us and deliver us from our troubles (see Psalm 54). It is our Christian duty not to worry about God exacting justice but to trust God for our own deliverance. Remember, in all good time, justice will be done.

Tale VIII. THE VISITOR

We've all heard the adage that "No one is ever really alone," but how many of us actually believe that? After all, there is another well-known saying that states, "When it comes our time to die, each of us dies alone, whether people are there with us or not."

Death can be such a terrifying thing, so full of unanswered questions. And it is our nature as humans that we don't deal well with things we don't fully understand.

When I wrote this story, I purposely left the old woodcutter nameless because he stands for each and every one of us in our supposed independence and our seeming aloneness. Despite his rugged independence, he finds himself faced with the unavoidable — death — a fate which comes to all, even the righteous (see Wisdom 18:20). Although he'd had a long and full life, the grim prospect of its end is before the woodcutter, and it robs him of his peace of heart. No one is so secure or happy that the shadow of death does not cause him or her some degree of fear or discomfort. After all, what waits beyond is very uncertain. And even though life in this world may sometimes be happy, the Bible cautions us:

> Call no man happy before his death,
>   for by how he ends, a man is known.
>
> (Sirach 11:28)

Beyond this earthly life lies the unsure fate awaiting us on the other side of death's door. Death is a crossing that we seemingly make alone.

But are we really alone at that moment? On the eve of his death Jesus told his disciples, "I am not alone, because the Father is with me. I have told you this so that you might have peace in me. In the world you will have trouble, but take courage, I have conquered the world" (John 16:32-33). These words assure us that Jesus and God are always there for us and with us, and we can be certain that this promise holds true at the moment of death as well. If we are united to Christ, then we are united to God through him. There can never be a moment in which Christ is not present to us, and he would certainly not abandon us at the hour of our greatest terror.

But there is more: Jesus promised us that after he had returned to the Father he would send us another comforter to help us and be with us in our trials and agonies. This helper, or *Paraclete* ("Clete," get it?), gives us encouragement and moral comfort to see us through difficult times. (In some biblical translations the Paraclete is instead called *Advocate*.) In the woodcutter's story little Clete was indeed the Comforter Jesus promised to send to us all (see John 14:16). When would we ever need the Comforter more than at the hour of our death? This Comforter is admirably equipped to aid us in our need, for as Jesus said at the Last Supper, "When the Advocate comes...the Spirit of truth that proceeds from the Father, he will testify to me" (John 15:26). At the moment of our death the most important truth that the Paraclete will utter to us is that Christ has ended the power of death and through the gospel has revealed immortal life (see 2 Timothy 1:10). If you ever find yourself frozen in fear, remember the words of the psalmist,

> Even though I walk in the dark valley
>   I fear no evil; for you are at my side
> With your rod and your staff
>   that give me courage.

> (Psalm 23:4)

If we add to this the comfort of praying with the Mother of God the words in the Hail Mary, ("...now and at the hour of our death. Amen.") then we are indeed hardly alone but traveling in very good company on the journey out of this life.

Alone? Hardly!

So that being said, none of us will ever have any fears or doubts about the life to come, right? Well, for most of us, no. It's the human condition to worry and fret, and we all like to have the sword of firm fact to slay the dragon of doubt. We don't have those facts, proven and beyond doubt, when it comes to questions and answers about the hereafter. But we *do* have the testimony of one who has himself conquered death and who assures us, "God gave us eternal life, and this life is in his Son" (1 John 5:11). If we have faith in that testimony, that faith will slay our fears, for our God is a God who does not lie.

Tale IX. HANNAH OF SOROKI

Once again the theme of this tale revolves around prejudice, but the difference is that this tale specifically addresses the form of prejudice that I feel is the most displeasing of all to God — religious prejudice. In the Bible there are numerous condemnations of the heathen religions found in ancient Israel, but these were religions that not only honored false gods but also practiced particularly horrible rituals, such as child sacrifice (see Leviticus 18:21 and 20:1-5). The penalty for this type of worship demanded death according to Jewish law. It was a sin that was not confined to heathens, however, for even King Ahaz of Judah sinned in this way (see 2 Kings 16:1-3). Failure to worship Yahweh alone was the real issue here. Sadly, it often happened that the Israelites gave way to such practices.

In the Book of Ezra we read about how intermarriage with other peoples was forbidden for the Israelites, the underlying fear being that Israel would be contaminated by others' foreign gods and practices (see Ezra 9 and 10).

Nehemiah refused offers of help for rebuilding the walls of Jerusalem when the offers came from non-Jews. He said, "We, [God's] servants, shall set about the rebuilding; but for you there is to be neither share nor claim nor memorial in Jerusalem" (Nehemiah 2:20).

The roots of religious suspicion run deep when reinforced by negative encounters with people of other beliefs, and that is as true of our own day as it was then. Jesus opposed sin as much as Yahweh had, but Jesus did not accept it as an excuse to hate or persecute sinners.

The Samaritans of Jesus' time were despised by Jews who thought they were "better" Jews than the Samaritans were. Jesus encountered many Jews who thought the Samaritans were rivals to the claim of who were the "true" children of Israel. As a result *Samaritan* became a byword for all that was low and false. So bitter were the two groups' mutual hatred that the gospels tell of how Jews actually avoided traveling through Samaritan territory for fear of personal danger. We may assume Samaritans likewise avoided the "proper" Jews' land too. Despite this, Jesus used Samaritans to show us the proper way of relating to those whose beliefs are different from our own.

In the parable of The Good Samaritan, it is a hated Samaritan who does the godly thing by actually helping a battered man on the roadside (see Luke 10:25-37). In this parable Jesus has the nerve to say that the despised Samaritan was *really* the battered man's neighbor rather than the priest and the Levite (both religious men) who passed him by.

In the encounter with the Samaritan woman at Jacob's well, Jesus does not avoid talking to the woman whose people were supposedly deluded heretics. Instead he uses the occasion to preach God's truth to her and her townspeople (see John 4:1-41).

Even the apostles suffered from religious prejudice. One day the apostle John came to Jesus and said:

> "Teacher, we saw someone driving out demons in your name, and we tried to prevent him because he does not follow us." Jesus replied, "Do not prevent him. There is no one who performs a mighty deed in my name who can at the same time speak ill of me. For whoever is not against us is for us."
>
> (Mark 9:38-40)

In the story of Hannah (which I modeled after the Book of Judith) the heroine is a member of a despised religious minority. Yet she is the one who saves the town. Like the Good Samaritan, she sacrifices without thinking about who it is she helps. In the end the people celebrate their deliverance and mourn the loss of their deliverer without regard for her religious affiliation. This is truly Christlike — not only to recognize that our ways and expressions of worship may be different but also to recognize that we still worship the same God. Love doesn't demand agreement of belief on all particulars; it demands that we look past differences to see other human beings who are also made in God's image. We must respect such persons for who they are rather than hate them for what they believe. When we can do that, then our attitude is truly that of Christ.

Tale X. THE MIGHTY GORM

One of the finest things about the Book of Proverbs is how it can be noble and tactful at one moment and then in the next paragraph shift to blunt honesty that hits a person right in the gut.

So it is with the proverb that tells us the essence of Gorm's problem: It says, "He who trusts in himself is a fool" (Proverbs 28:26). There is no escaping this fact or rationalizing it away. Whenever we trust only our own strength, skill, wisdom, or power rather than that of God, we are setting ourselves up for a hard fall. When we trust ourselves alone, we lose perspective. That was the case in the story of David and Goliath. Goliath, smug in his sense of being number one, forgot that once you get to number one it can be tough to stay there. As a result, he underestimated his enemy and the rest is history (see 1 Samuel 17:32-51).

When we consistently fail to consider our own limitations, it can lead to disaster. No amount of saving money, eating right, exercising, car maintenance, getting good grades, and endless other preparations can offer us complete protection from disasters. Only God can offer real protection from disaster. To find a character similar to Gorm, read the parable of the Rich Fool, a man who was so smug and confident in his riches and comforts that he lost sight of the fact that he stood in danger of losing his soul (see Luke 12:16-21).

Many times God has spoken bluntly through the writers of Scripture. God has done this to remind us that we cannot completely trust riches, other human beings, military might, rulers, or any other earthly people or things. Only God, who has placed all these people and things on earth, is truly in control. God can withdraw support if people are not behaving justly and morally. Likewise, we must not trust any false idols (including money, fame, and power) because when we do, we substitute those things for God. If we really want to be blessed, we have only to put our trust where it properly belongs — in God.

In the Book of Ecclesiastes the writer begins his work with a lengthy reflection on how useless all of our efforts really are without God: "For to whatever man he sees fit he gives wisdom and knowledge and joy; but to the sinner he gives the task of gathering possessions to be given to whatever man God sees fit" (Ecclesiastes 2:26). In short, life becomes an empty frustration to those who put their trust only in earthly goods and people. The writer of Ecclesiastes urges us to revere and obey God's commands, for God will judge everything we do, good or bad, known or secret (see Ecclesiastes 12:13-14). No matter who we are or who we *think* we are, we cannot function without God.

Gorm, like many other "great" beings, had a firm faith in his own strength, will power, and ego. The famous philosopher Friedrich Nietzsche wrote about people's thirst for power over everything in their world. Nietzsche called it *the will to power*. The will to power has led many would-be stand-ins for God down a road to destruction. Adam and Eve were prime victims of the will to power when God warned them not to eat fruit from a tree that would give them knowledge of good and evil. They ate the fruit anyway because they wanted the power of knowledge that the tree would give them. The rest is history. This story further illustrates the fact that usually some small miscalculation or someone or something that "great" people regard as powerless to hurt them often ends up being their downfall. Alexander the Great conquered the known world in his time and stood at the height of his power and fame when he died suddenly after a long bout of too much eating and drinking.

Real greatness comes from doing God's will, and real power comes to us through God, and God alone. Perhaps the irony of it all is found in Jesus' words to his disciples, "The greatest among you must be your servant. Whoever exalts himself will be humbled; but whoever humbles himself will be exalted" (Matthew 23:11-12).

May we all become so great.

THE TALE OF SMALL AND DEEP *(Epilogue)*

The parable about the voices, Small and Deep demands a brief reflection. Gershom's telling of this parable is the "capstone" — the point he was building up to throughout all the tales. The story of Small and Deep contains the lesson he wants to leave with the pilgrim.

Jesus once told his disciples, "I say to you, unless a grain of wheat falls to the ground and dies, it remains just a grain of wheat; but if it dies, it produces much fruit" (John 12:24). The "death" of the grain of wheat is not bad because the grain is meant to be so much more. It is to give new life and pass the gift of life along! Likewise, the "death" of Small resulted in the birth of a beautiful flower.

We are all seeds containing the essence of something more that we are meant to be. But we never grow unless we decide to risk — to die to self, and chance it that our more glorious destiny will be realized. God plants potential splendor within each of us, but such splendor will never "see the sun" unless we choose to cultivate it and help it grow. We are not robots with all our actions predetermined and programmed into us. God has destined us all to glory in heaven if we choose to follow his ways, but we have the free will to choose to do otherwise. It may seem crazy to want anything else, but much of human history records peoples' decisions to turn from God because they thought they knew how to do things better than God did.

It is faith that allows us to be willing to die to self. It is not easy to die to self. It involves trading the security of who we presently are for the uncertainty of who we can be. But if we freely choose faith in God, we will find that we have embraced a destiny that God has prepared for us from the beginning — a marvelous and joyous existence beyond anything we could possibly imagine.

I hope these tales have opened possibilities to you who have read or heard them. May they help you find the faith to be all that God means you to be. Like Mary, the Mother of Jesus, I hope you have the courage to say, "May it be done to me according to your word" (Luke 1:38).

God bless you, pilgrims.

Brother Stephen